Unit I - Introduction to Job-Related Thinking Skills... 1

Pretest for Manual of Job-Related Thinking Skills.. *3*

Unit II - Deductive Reasoning -- *Empowering the Mind*.. 7

Introduction to Deductive Reasoning *7*

Part II.A. Reasoning With Two Sets *9*
   Section II.A.1. What Are Sets?... 9
   Section II.A.2. The Four Basic Statements About Sets....................................... 10
   Section II.A.3. Conclusions From "All Are" Statements 14
   Section II.A.4. Conclusions From "None Are" Statements................................. 17
   Section II.A.5. Conclusions From "Some Are" Statements 19
   Section II.A.6. Conclusions From "Some Are Not" Statements 21
   Section II.A.7. Conclusions When the Basic Statements Are False..................... 24

Part II.B Reasoning with Three Sets.. *29*
   Section II.B.1. Forms for Relating Three Sets... 29
   Section II.B.2. Advanced Topic -- Syllogistic Rules (reading this section is optional)35
   Section II.B.3. Illogical Biases in Relating Three Sets.. 37

Part II.C. Reasoning with Connectives... *39*
   Section II.C.1. Conjunction and Negation... 40
   Section II.C.2. The Conditional 43
   Section II.C.3. Other Basic Connectives 48
   Section II.C.4. Advanced Topic -- Complex Connectives 52

Part II.D. Using Language Correctly in Deduction.. *55*

Unit III. Induction 1 -- Reasoning About Real-World Events **57**

Part III.A. Introduction to Inductive Reasoning... *57*

Part III.B. Inductive Reasoning About Sets.. *61*
   Section III.B.1: Inductive Reasoning About Two Sets... 61
   Section III.B.2. Advanced Topic -- Inductive Reasoning With More Than Two Sets.. 67

Table of Contents	Page

Part III.C. Inductive Reasoning With Connectives.. 70
  Section III.C.1: Conditionals With Probabilities.. 70
  Section III.C.2: Connectives With an Added Premise Containing a Probability 73

Part III.D. Fallacies in Induction... 78

Unit IV - Induction 2: Statistical Reasoning and Estimating Probability 80

Part IV.A. Populations and Samples 80
  Section IV.A.1. Law of Large Numbers.. 81
  Section IV.A.2. Sample Representativeness... 83
  Section IV.A.3. Regression to the Mean 85
  Section IV.A.4. Sample Validity 87
  Section IV.A.5. Summary... 88

Part IV.B. Estimating Probability 89
  Section IV.B.1. Probability Defined... 89
  Section IV.B.2. Base Rate Information and Probability Estimates 89
  Section IV.B.3. Occurrence of Two or More Events 90
  Section IV.B.4. Multiplicative Rules of Probability.. 90
  Section IV.B.5. Additive Rules of Probability 93
  Section IV.B.6. Summary... 95

Part IV.C. Biases in Statistical Reasoning and Estimations of Probability . 96
  Section IV.C.1. Availability 96
  Section IV.C.2. Representativeness.. 96
  Section IV.C.3. Dilution 97
  Section IV.C.4. Anchoring and Adjustment.. 97
  Section IV.C.5. Order Effect 98
  Section IV.C.6. Ignoring Relative Frequency 99
  Section IV.C.7. Concrete Information.. 99
  Section IV.C.8. Gambler's Fallacy 100
  Section IV.C.9. Misperceptions about Equiprobability... 100
  Section IV.C.10. Overestimating Conjunctive Events 101
  Section IV.C.11. Summary... 102

Unit V - Posttest for Manual of Job-Related Thinking Skills.. 103

Unit II - Answers to Self Tests 111

Unit I - Introduction to Job-Related Thinking Skills

A Border Patrol Agent deciding whether an impending confrontation involves dangerous individuals, an Inspector determining if an alien should be admitted, a supervisory Special Agent deciding whether to open a case based on certain evidence -- all of these are DHS employees using their thinking skills. Every day, DHS employees use their thinking skills in countless decisions, determinations, and investigations. Thinking skills are by no means the only skills used by DHS employees, but they are the most important. They are used in applying rules, making determinations, making predictions, and in problem solving, on-the-spot decision making, and complex, deliberate decision making.

In spite of the importance of thinking skills, most people do not receive special training in thinking. Employees receive training in job knowledge and supervisors usually receive training in supervisory techniques. Those types of training help employees think about very specific problems. By contrast, the purpose of this module is to teach **general** thinking skills that can be applied to any subject or situation.

In college programs, thinking skills are taught in logic courses. In addition, courses in research methods and statistics teach people how to collect and analyze data in order to draw correct conclusions. This manual draws heavily on the parts of logic and statistical reasoning that are useful to DHS employees.

Which Job-Related Thinking Skills Are Included in This Manual?

The first skills in this manual are the basic thinking skills, which can be called **deduction** and **induction**. These are the two types of skills that are used in drawing conclusions from given information. Deduction and induction are very similar. They differ in only two ways-- the completeness of the available information and the degree of certainty of the conclusion, as indicated below:

- Deduction: The individual has all the information necessary to draw a conclusion. The conclusion is certain; it is true if the evidence is true.

- Induction: The individual does not have complete evidence. He or she draws a conclusion based on the information available. The conclusion is uncertain, that is to say, probabilistic; it may not be true even if the evidence is true.

In the work of DHS, deduction is typically used in applying laws and rules to specific situations. Induction is used in situations in which officers need to make on-the-spot probabilistic judgments, sometimes in life-threatening situations.

Statistical reasoning is a tool to help us draw conclusions when we do not have complete information. We can think of statistical reasoning as a powerful aid to induction.

Throughout this manual, there will be tips to help you avoid common mistakes of reasoning (these mistakes are called *fallacies*). In addition, some sections contain *Logic Notes* that give you more detail about logical issues. You do not need to read these notes in order to understand the rest of the manual, but you are encouraged to do so. In addition, there are a number of sections that contain *Advanced Topics*, which are more difficult topics. If you have time to study these topics, you are encouraged to do so. However, you do not need to study these topics to understand the rest of the manual. At the back of the manual, there is a *Glossary of Key Terms* that you should refer to whenever you want to know the meaning of a term that is defined elsewhere in the manual.

How Should You Use This Training Manual?

This manual is designed for self-instruction. The information is presented in small sections that you can study separately. At the end of each section, there is a Self-Test that you should take in order to check your understanding of the material you have studied. It is very important that you answer all of these questions and then study the answers to the questions. The answers to these exercises are found at the end of the manual. On the side of each page of answers, there are one, two, three, four, or five lines (like this ▬) which indicate that the answers belong to Unit I, II, III, IV, or V. If you think you may want to work through the manual a second time, you may wish to write your answers to the Self-Tests on a separate piece of paper so that when you go back to review, the answers will not be already filled in.

Self-Test: Unit I (answers are given on page 107)

For each of the statements below, decide which of the two words in parentheses makes the statement a true statement.

1. Deduction and induction are (basic, advanced) types of thinking skills.

2. Deduction is the type of reasoning that leads to a (certain, probabilistic) conclusion.

3. Deductive conclusions are based on (incomplete, complete) evidence.

4. Induction is the type of reasoning that leads to a (certain, probabilistic) conclusion.

5. Inductive conclusions are based on (incomplete, complete) evidence.

6. Statistical reasoning is an aid to (deduction, induction).

Before studying the rest of the manual, take this 32-question pretest and check your answers (answers begin on page 107). At the end of the manual, there is a posttest that you can take to assess your improvement.

Pretest for Manual of Job-Related Thinking Skills

The following passage describes a set of facts. The passage is followed by eight conclusions. Read the passage and then decide whether each conclusion is:

T) **true**, *which means that you can infer the conclusion from the facts given; or*

F) **false**, *which means that the conclusion is contrary to the facts given; or whether there is*

I) **insufficient information to decide**, *which means that there is insufficient information for you to determine whether the facts imply the conclusion or are contrary to the conclusion.*

All narcotics cases resulting from apprehensions by the Border Patrol are referred to the Drug Enforcement Administration (DEA); narcotics cases are the only cases referred to DEA by the Border Patrol. At Station X, last month was unusual in that none of the criminal cases resulting from apprehensions by the Border Patrol were narcotics cases. A few of the criminal cases resulting from apprehensions that month involved alien smuggling, and these were not referred to another agency.

1. Last month, there were no narcotics cases among the criminal cases that resulted from apprehensions by the Border Patrol in Station X. (T / F / I)

2. Last month, some of the criminal cases resulting from apprehensions by the Border Patrol in Station X were referred to another agency. (T / F / I)

3. Last month, none of the criminal cases resulting from apprehensions in Station X were referred to the DEA. (T / F / I)

4. Any case that is not referred to DEA is not a narcotics case. (T / F / I)

5. A few of the criminal cases resulting from apprehensions by the Border Patrol in Station X last month were narcotics cases. (T / F / I)

6. There are no narcotics cases resulting from apprehensions by the Border Patrol that are not referred to the DEA. (T / F / I)

7. There were some cases that were referred to another agency last month that were not criminal cases. (T / F / I)

8. Last month, there were some alien smuggling cases resulting from apprehensions by the Border Patrol in Station X that did not involve narcotics. (T / F / I)

The following passage describes a set of facts. The passage is followed by eight conclusions. Read the passage and then decide whether each conclusion is:

T) **true**, *which means that you can infer the conclusion from the facts given; or*

F) **false**, *which means that the conclusion is contrary to the facts given; or whether there is*

I) **insufficient information to decide**, *which means that there is insufficient information for you to determine whether the facts imply the conclusion or are contrary to the conclusion.*

If aliens do not present themselves for inspection at a designated port of entry, they cannot enter the U.S.A. legally. In order to enter, the alien must have either a border crossing card or a resident alien card or a passport. During a specific one-week period, records at one port of entry showed that if an alien had a border crossing card, he or she was either visiting family members or entering to shop. One individual, J.T., entered at this port of entry during this week with a border crossing card. J.T. was not entering to shop in the U.S.A.

9. An alien who does not have a border crossing card would need to present a resident alien card or a passport to enter the U.S.A. legally. (T / F / I)

10. If an alien entered the U.S.A. legally, then that alien must have presented himself or herself at a designated port of entry. (T / F / I)

11. Another alien, M.N., presented herself at the designated port of entry; therefore, she was allowed to enter. (T / F / I)

12. During the one-week period referred to in the paragraph, if an alien who entered through this port of entry was shopping in the U.S.A., that person had presented a border crossing card. (T / F / I)

13. J.T. entered at the port of entry to visit his family. (T / F / I)

14. J.T. can enter the U.S.A. legally without presenting himself at the port of entry. (T / F / I)

15. During the one-week period referred to in the paragraph, any alien who entered at this port of entry without a border crossing card was not visiting family. (T / F / I)

16. During this one week period, if an alien did not present himself or herself at this port of entry, he or she did not have either a border crossing card or a resident alien card or a passport. (T / F / I)

The following passage describes a set of facts. The passage is followed by eight conclusions. Read the passage and then decide whether each conclusion is:

T) **true**, *which means that you can infer the conclusion from the facts given; or*

F) **false**, *which means that the conclusion is contrary to the facts given; or whether there is*

I) **insufficient information to decide**, *which means that there is insufficient information for you to determine whether the facts imply the conclusion or are contrary to the conclusion.*

An illegal alien can either take voluntary departure or be deported, but not both. In a one-month period in Sector X, all apprehensions of illegal aliens were of people who subsequently took voluntary departure. During this period, there were several apprehensions that involved extensive pursuit by local authorities. Three of these cases involved pursuit to the same crossroads. At this crossroads, the road straight ahead was visible for a mile. A left turn at this crossroads led to a road that was hidden from view. There was no right turn at the crossroads. Therefore, in all three cases, when local officers lost sight of the person they were pursuing just before coming to the crossroads, they knew that the individual had either turned left, or been picked up by a vehicle, or both. In summarizing the cases after all three were apprehended, the local authorities concluded that only one of the individuals was picked up by a vehicle.

Evaluate these conclusions with respect to Sector X in this one-month time period.

17. Some cases that required extensive pursuit by local authorities resulted in the voluntary departure of aliens. (T / F / I)

18. Some apprehended aliens were deported. (T / F / I)

19. All apprehensions of illegal aliens occurred as the result of an extensive pursuit by local authorities. (T / F / I)

20. In at least two of the cases that were pursued to the crossroads, the individuals being pursued took the left turn. (T / F / I)

21. There were some pursuits by local authorities that led to apprehensions of illegal aliens. (T / F / I)

22. Every person who took voluntary departure was apprehended after an extensive pursuit by local authorities. (T / F / I)

23. Some apprehensions did not occur without an extensive pursuit by local authorities. (T / F / I)

24. One of the individuals pursued to the crossroads did not turn left and was not picked up by a vehicle. (T / F / I)

The following passage describes a set of facts. The passage is followed by eight conclusions. Read the passage and then decide whether each conclusion is:

T) **true**, *which means that you can infer the conclusion from the facts given; or*

F) **false**, *which means that the conclusion is contrary to the facts given, or whether there is*

I) **insufficient information to decide**, *which means that there is insufficient information for you to determine whether the facts imply the conclusion or are contrary to the conclusion.*

A railroad bridge that crosses the U.S. border has a catwalk for workers that is used by aliens to enter the U.S.A. illegally. A special sensor installed on the bridge alerts Border Patrol Agents to the presence of people on the bridge when no train is present. If there is no train, 70% of sensor signals (so-called "hits") produce apprehensions of at least one new illegal alien. When a train is present, it masks the sensor hits. Apprehensions are made when a train is present, but the sensor is not a useful tool for signaling the presence of people.

In an average week, there are 100 sensor hits in the absence of trains and 10 apprehensions in the presence of trains. A group of illegal aliens, which we will call group A, was apprehended while crossing the railroad bridge. Another group, group B, crossed the bridge but was not apprehended.

25. If an illegal alien crosses the bridge and activates the sensor when a train is present, the probability is .10 that the alien will be apprehended. (T / F / I)

26. If a Border Patrol Agent responds to a sensor hit when no train is present, there is a 70% chance that an alien will be apprehended. (T / F / I)

27. More likely than not, Group B crossed the railroad bridge when the train was present. (T / F / I)

28. It is very likely that Group A crossed the railroad bridge when the train was not present. (T / F / I)

29. Trains are present at this bridge approximately 10% of the time. (T / F / I)

30. It is not true that no apprehensions occur when a train is present. (T / F / I)

31. When a train is not present, a sensor hit is certain to produce an apprehension of an illegal alien. (T / F / I)

32. More illegal aliens attempted to cross the bridge when no train was present than when a train was present. (T / F / I)

End of Pretest. Check your answers against those on pages 107-110.

Unit II - Deductive Reasoning -- *Empowering the Mind*

Introduction to Deductive Reasoning

Deductive reasoning empowers your mind because it allows you to draw conclusions that are certain, that is, conclusions that must be true if they are based on true information. This can help you on your job because much of the work of DHS employees involves deductive activities such as applying rules and making determinations.

The term *valid conclusion* means a conclusion that is justified, given the evidence. A conclusion that is not justified is called an *invalid conclusion*.

Training in deductive reasoning teaches you to recognize several types of simple sentences or statements and to understand which conclusions can be drawn from them. This may sound like an academic exercise, but it is not. These simple sentences correspond to real-life situations.

The following example shows you a simple statement and a sample of the valid conclusions that can be drawn from it. There is also a sample of invalid conclusions--conclusions that cannot be drawn from the statement. Study these sentences and be sure that you understand why statements 1a and 1b are valid conclusions from statement 1. Also be sure you understand why statements 1c and 1d are invalid conclusions from statement 1.

Statement 1.	All DHS employees are employees of the Federal Government.

Valid conclusions
Statement 1a.	Some employees of the Federal Government are DHS employees.
Statement 1b.	Anyone who is not an employee of the Federal Government is not a DHS employee.

Invalid conclusions
Statement 1c.	No employees of the Federal Government are DHS employees.
Statement 1d.	Some DHS employees are not employees of the Federal Government.

Statement 1 is an example of a sentence that has the following basic form:

Statement 2.   All [members of category A] are [members of category B].

In statement 1 above, "DHS employees" are the members of category A and "employees of the Federal Government" are the members of category B.

Any statement that has the same form as statement 2 will have the same pattern of valid conclusions as statements 1a and 1b and the same pattern of invalid conclusions as statements 1c and 1d. These patterns, illustrated in terms of category A and category B, are as follows:

Statement 2.	All [members of category A] are [members of category B].
Valid conclusions	
Statement 2a.	Some [members of category B] are [members of category A].
Statement 2b.	All [nonmembers of category B] are [nonmembers of category A].
Invalid conclusions	
Statement 2c.	No [members of category B] are [members of category A].
Statement 2d.	Some [members of category A] are not [members of category B].

In the rest of Unit II, you will learn about many other forms for statements that permit valid deductive conclusions. You will also learn how to combine information from two or more statements to reach valid conclusions.

Self-Test: Introduction to Deductive Reasoning (answers are given on page 111)

1. A deductive conclusion is true if it is based on true evidence. (True / false)

2. A conclusion that is not justified, given the evidence, is invalid. (True / false)

3. From the statement *All guns are weapons*, write one valid conclusion (like 2a or 2b):

4. From the statement *All guns are weapons*, write one invalid conclusion (like 2c or 2d):

Questions 5 through 8 use nonsense words in order to let you answer the questions strictly on the basis of the logical form, without being influenced by your prior knowledge.

If the statement *All gorms are lames* is true, which of the following conclusions are valid?

5. Some gorms are not lames. (Valid / invalid)

6. Some lames are gorms. (Valid / invalid)

7. No lames are gorms. (Valid / invalid)

8. All non-lames are non-gorms. (Valid / invalid)

Part II.A. Reasoning With Two Sets

The best starting place for learning about deduction is with sentences that show the relationship between two sets or two categories, like the sentences in the preceding section. Before we talk more about sentences, though, we should be sure the term *set* is clear to you.

Section II.A.1. What Are Sets?

Sets are groupings of individuals or things that share one or more characteristics. The following words can be considered to represent sets:

laws	vehicles	Border Patrol Agents
agencies	employees	cases

The following lists show words and phrases that are not sets (left column) and a way of rewriting them as a phrase that expresses a set (right column). As you can see, words that express a characteristic can be changed into sets by adding a noun such as "things" or "individuals."

Not Sets	Sets
Green	green things
Illegal	illegal aliens or illegal acts
Detained	detained individuals
crossed the border	people who crossed the border

Frequently sentences refer to sets implicitly rather than explicitly. These sentences can be rewritten to show explicitly the relationship between sets. The following is an example:

Statement 3a.   All supervisors *will attend training this year*.

Statement 3b.   All supervisors are *employees who will attend training this year*.

In statement 3a, the italicized portion is not written in terms of a set. In statement 3b, the italicized portion is rewritten to express a set. Notice that the content of the two sentences is essentially the same.[1]

Statements 4a and 4b illustrate the same point:

---

[1] **Logic Note.** The subject of the sentence is usually one of the sets and the predicate of the sentence usually represents the other set. You will notice that the italicized portion of sentences 3a and 4a are the predicates of their sentences. These portions are rewritten as sets in sentences 3b and 4b.

Statement 4a.   Some illegal immigrants *live in Texas*.

Statement 4b.   Some illegal immigrants are *people who live in Texas*.

Self-Test: Section II.A.1 (answers are given on page 111)

In 1 through 5, decide if the word or phrase expresses a set. If it does not, change the word or phrase so that it expresses a set.

                                                                    If not a set, rewrite:

1. listening   (Set / not a set)

2. District Directors   (Set / not a set)

3. hazardous   (Set / not a set)

4. completed and filed   (Set / not a set)

5. regular working hours (Set / not a set)

Each sentence in 6 through 10 below refers to two sets. What are the two sets referred to in each sentence? Underline the two sets. In each sentence, rewrite the second set so that it is expressed in set language. Refer to statements 3a and 3b and 4a and 4b for examples.

6. Some computer software is user-friendly.

7. Some law enforcement personnel carry guns.

8. Some Mexicans were deported.

9. All Border Patrol Agents speak Spanish.

10. All service employees are responsible for immediately reporting any allegation of misconduct.

Section II.A.2. The Four Basic Statements About Sets

There are four basic statements about the relationships between two sets. In this section we will show you what these four statements are like. In subsequent sections, we will show you what types of conclusions you can draw from them.

These statements represent basic types of information that you receive on the job. From this information, you must draw conclusions, make decisions, and take actions. You want to be sure that your conclusions, decisions, and actions are correct, based on the information you have. We will show you what conclusions are justified from the four basic statements below.

To illustrate the four statements, we will use an example of information that you might receive about whether or not the new cars in your office's fleet were available for use in a particular month. The four possible statements are as follows:

- All of our new fleet cars are available for use this month.

- None of our new fleet cars are available for use this month.

- Some of our new fleet cars are available for use this month.

- Some of our new fleet cars are not available for use this month.

To give you a picture of what these statements mean, we will use diagrams in which circles represent complete sets. Figure 1a below is a possible representation of the statement "All of our new fleet cars are available for use this month." As you can see, all of the set "our new fleet cars" is included in the set "vehicles available for use this month." This captures the essential information in the statement, namely, that every new fleet car is available for use this month. Figure 1a, however, does not depict the only possible meaning of the statement "All of our new fleet cars are available for use this month." Figure 1b shows the other possible meaning, namely, that the two sets -- our new fleet cars and vehicles that are available for use this month -- overlap completely. If we only have the information "All of our new fleet cars are available for use this month," we do not know whether Figure 1a or 1b is the correct representation of the relationship between the two sets.

In the rest of this manual, we will use a diagram like Figure 1a to represent this type of statement. However, you should bear in mind that a diagram like Figure 1b might represent the true relationship between the two sets.

Figure 1a. Diagram for "All of our new fleet cars are available for use this month."

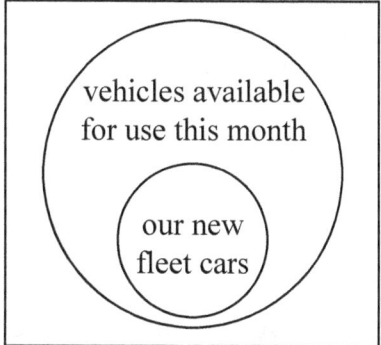

Figure 1b. Another Possible Meaning of "All of our new fleet cars are available for use this month."

12

Figure 2 below represents the statement "None of our new fleet cars are available for use this month." As you can see, there is no overlap of the two sets. All of the set "our new fleet cars" is outside all of the set "vehicles available for use this month."

Figure 2. Diagram for "None of our new fleet cars are available for use this month."

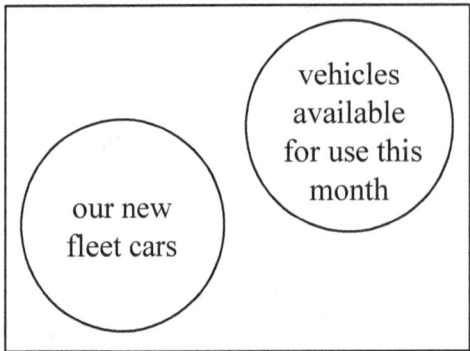

To illustrate the statement "Some of our new fleet cars are available for use this month," we will need a symbol to represent **part** of a set. We will use a semicircle to represent part of a set. Just as the word "some" has a very indefinite meaning, so you should also consider the semicircle to represent an undefined proportion of the set. In order to emphasize this, we have drawn the semicircle with a dashed line on one side.

Figure 3 illustrates the statement "Some of our new fleet cars are available for use this month." The diagram shows that some of the new fleet cars are available for use this month, but it does not give any information about the rest of the new fleet cars. That is to say, it does not give any information about what proportion of the new fleet cars are available for use this month.

Figure 3. Diagram for "Some of our new fleet cars are available for use this month."

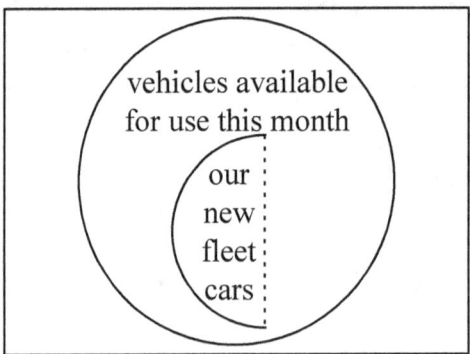

Figure 4 below illustrates the statement "Some of our new fleet cars are not available for use this month." As you can see, part of the set "our new fleet cars" is outside of the set "vehicles available for use this month." This diagram should be interpreted as not telling us

13

definitively if any of our new fleet cars are **inside** the circle for "vehicles available for use this month." We only know that some of them are **outside** the circle.

Figure 4. Diagram for "Some of our new fleet cars are not available for use this month."

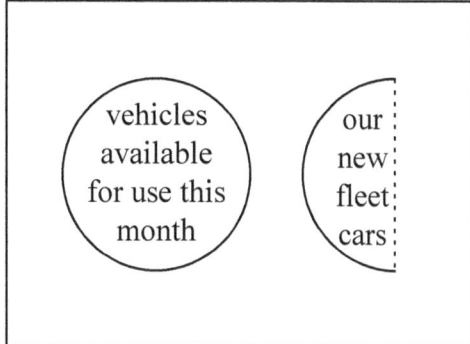

Self-Test: Section II.A.2 (answers are given on page 111)

Using circles to represent complete sets and semicircles to represent parts of sets, draw a diagram to illustrate the relationship of the sets in each of the statements below.

1. Every supervisory training course is filled to capacity for the next three months.

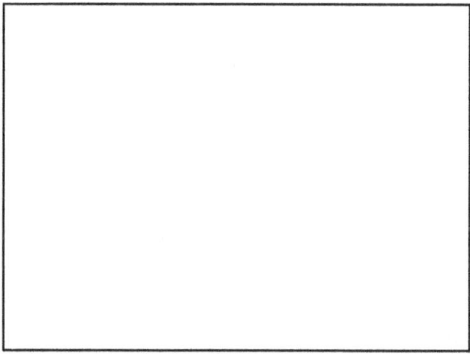

2. Some of the cases being handled by this office are very old.

3. None of the old computers is equipped with Windows software.

4. A few computers on our system are not working.

Section II.A.3. Conclusions From "All Are" Statements

If you have information that one set is totally included in another, such as "All of our new fleet cars are available for use this month," there are several conclusions that you can draw from that information and several conclusions that you cannot draw. We will discuss these conclusions as *true* conclusions, *false* conclusions, and conclusions for which there is *insufficient information*. True conclusions are the same as valid conclusions, but invalid conclusions either can be false or can be conclusions for which there is insufficient information.

True Conclusions

The following three important true conclusions can be drawn from the statement "All of our new fleet cars are available for use this month."

- Some vehicles that are available for use this month are our new fleet cars.

Explanation: Given that *all* of our new fleet cars are available for use this month, it follows that there are some vehicles that are available for use this month that are our new fleet cars.

15

- Any car that is not available for use this month is not one of our new fleet cars.

Explanation: Given that all of our new fleet cars are available for use this month, it follows that any car that is not available for use this month cannot be one of our new fleet cars. This can be seen by referring back to Figure 1a, the diagram of "All of our new fleet cars are available for use this month." Clearly, anything that is outside of the set of vehicles that are available for use this month is also outside the set of our new fleet cars.[2]

- None of our new fleet cars is unavailable for use this month.

Explanation: This true conclusion represents a double negation of the original statement. We have negated the verb of the sentence and we have negated the set "vehicles available for use this month." In other words, instead of saying "All of our new fleet cars are vehicles that are available for use this month," we are saying "*None* of our new fleet cars are *un*available for use this month." One negation cancels out the other. Therefore, the sentence says the same thing as the original statement.[3]

False Conclusions

The following two conclusions are clearly false if the statement "All of our new fleet cars are available for use this month" is true.

- None of our new fleet cars are available for use this month.

- Some of our new fleet cars are not available for use this month.

Explanation: These two conclusions are contrary to the meaning of the original statement.

A Conclusion for Which There Is Insufficient Information

The following conclusion is uncertain if the statement "All of our new fleet cars are available for use this month" is true.

- All of the vehicles that are available for use this month are our new fleet cars.

Explanation: This conclusion is uncertain because, although we know that the set of our new fleet cars is completely included in the set of vehicles that are available for use this month, we do not have enough information to know if the two sets are *identical*. The conclusion above would only be true if the two sets were identical. You may recall that

---

[2] **Logic Note**: This true conclusion represents a logical form called the *contrapositive*. The positions of the two sets in the original statement are reversed and the two sets are negated. Another example is as follows: For the statement "All guns are weapons" the true contrapositive would be "Anything that is not a weapon is not a gun."

[3] **Logic Note**: This true conclusion represents a logical form known as the *obverse*.

Figures 1a and 1b in the previous section represented the two possible meanings of "All are" statements. Without obtaining more information, we cannot tell which of these meanings is correct, and thus we cannot draw the uncertain conclusion given above.

The relationship between the original statement and the uncertain conclusion is shown in the following formulaic sentences. The original statement says:

All [members of set A] are [members of set B].

The uncertain conclusion says:

All [members of set B] are [members of set A].

You can see that the positions of the two sets are exchanged in the second sentence. In logic, the second sentence is called the *converse* of the first sentence.

Later in this unit you will see that some basic statements do have valid converses -- converses that mean the same thing as the original statement. It is important to know that the converse of a statement such as "All of our new fleet cars are available for use this month" cannot be concluded with certainty. However, it is very common for people to assume that this conclusion is valid. This reasoning mistake is so common that it has been called an *illogical bias* by authors who have studied the fallacies of human reasoning.

In the exercises that follow in the Self-Test, you will be asked to evaluate the correctness of various conclusions. Be especially careful to try to avoid the illogical bias referred to above. It is a bias you should always avoid, particularly when making inferences and decisions on the job.

Self-Test: Section II.A.3 (answers are given on page 113)

In the questions below, you will be given a statement that is followed by four conclusions. Given that the statement is true, you should indicate whether each conclusion is *true* (you can infer the conclusion from the statement) or *false* (you can infer that the conclusion is contrary to the statement), or if there is *insufficient information to decide* whether the conclusion is true or false.

1. All members of our staff have mailboxes at the front desk.

    a. Some members of our staff do not have mailboxes at the front desk. (T / F / I)

    b. Some people who have mailboxes at the front desk are members of our staff. (T / F / I)

    c. All people who have mailboxes at the front desk are members of our staff. (T / F / I)

d. Anyone who does not have a mailbox at the front desk is not a member of our staff. (T / F / I)

2. Every supervisory training course is filled to capacity for the next three months.

   a. The only courses that are filled to capacity for the next three months are the supervisory training courses. (T / F / I)

   b. No supervisory training courses are filled to capacity for the next three months. (T / F / I)

   c. None of the supervisory training courses is filled to less than capacity for the next three months. (T / F / I)

   d. Any course in the next three months that is not filled to capacity is not a supervisory training course. (T / F / I)

Section II.A.4. Conclusions From "None Are" Statements

A statement such as "None of our new fleet cars are available for use this month" indicates that there is no overlap between the two sets in the statement. In other words, the first set, "our new fleet cars," is completely excluded from the set "vehicles that are available for use this month." Given this relationship between the two sets, there are two conclusions you can draw as well as two conclusions you cannot draw. We will discuss these as *true* conclusions and *false* conclusions.

True Conclusions

The following two true conclusions can be drawn from the statement "None of our new fleet cars are available for use this month."

- No vehicle that is available for use this month is one of our new fleet cars.

Explanation: Since vehicles that are available for use this month are totally excluded from the set of our new fleet cars, any car that is available for use this month cannot be one of our new fleet cars. You may recognize this conclusion as having the form of the *converse*, which is the form in which the positions of the two sets in the sentence are exchanged.

You may recall that the converse was not a valid conclusion from the statement "All of our new fleet cars are available for use this month." However, you can see that the converse is a valid conclusion from the statement "None of our new fleet cars are available for use this month." It is valid because the two sets are totally separated from each other. Figure 2 on page 12 illustrates the separation of the two sets.

- All of our new fleet cars are unavailable for use this month.

18

Explanation: This true conclusion represents a double negation of the original statement, "None of our new fleet cars are available for use this month" ("All" replaces "None" and "unavailable for use this month" replaces "available for use this month"). It has the same meaning as the original statement because the two negatives cancel each other out.[4]

When we negate a set, we can use the prefix "non" or another prefix, such as "dis," "im," "in," or "un," or we can use other wording that indicates that the set is negated. For example, if we were negating the set of "proper things," we could call that set "improper things." In the example we have been using above, we used "unavailable for use this month" to negate the set "available for use this month."

False Conclusions

The following two conclusions are clearly false if the statement "None of our new fleet cars are available for use this month" is true.

- All of our new fleet cars are available for use this month.

- Some of our new fleet cars are available for use this month.

Explanation: These two conclusions are contrary to the meaning of the original statement.

Self-Test: Section II.A.4 (answers are given on page 113)

In the questions below, you will be given a statement that is followed by four conclusions. Given that the statement is true, you should indicate whether each conclusion is *true* (you can infer the conclusion from the statement) or *false* (you can infer that the conclusion is contrary to the statement), or if there is *insufficient information to decide* whether the conclusion is true or false.

1. None of the new Jeeps are being deployed to Station 1.

   a. Some of the new Jeeps are being deployed to Station 1. (T / F / I)

   b. None of the vehicles being deployed to Station 1 is a new Jeep. (T / F / I)

   c. All of the new Jeeps are among the vehicles that are not being deployed to Station 1. (T / F / I)

   d. All of the new Jeeps are being deployed to Station 1. (T / F / I)

---

[4] **Logic Note.** You may recall from the previous section that this form is called the *obverse*.

2. None of the Assistant Chiefs will be able to attend the meeting.

    a. All of the Assistant Chiefs will be able to attend the meeting. (T / F / I)

    b. None of the people who will be able to attend the meeting are Assistant Chiefs. (T / F / I)

    c. Some of the people who will be able to attend the meeting are Assistant Chiefs. (T / F / I)

    d. All of the Assistant Chiefs will be unable to attend the meeting. (T / F / I)

Section II.A.5. Conclusions From "Some Are" Statements

A statement such as "Some of our new fleet cars are available for use this month" indicates that there are at least some members of one set that are included in the other set. From this information, there are two *true* conclusions that you can draw and one *false* conclusion that you cannot draw. In addition, there are two conclusions that you cannot draw because you have *insufficient information.*

True Conclusions

The following two true conclusions can be drawn from the statement "Some of our new fleet cars are available for use this month."

- Some vehicles that are available for use this month are our new fleet cars.

Explanation: Since some of our new fleet cars are available for use this month, it is clear that there are some vehicles that are available for use this month that are our new fleet cars. Perhaps you recognize that this form is the *converse,* the form in which the positions of the two sets in the sentence are exchanged. The converse is a valid conclusion from a statement that some members of one set are members of another set.

- Some of our new fleet cars are not unavailable for use this month.

Explanation: This true conclusion represents a double negation of the original statement "Some of our new fleet cars are available for use this month." It has the same meaning as the original statement because the two negatives cancel each other out.[5]

---

[5] **Logic Note.** You may recall that this form is called the *obverse.*

False Conclusion

The following conclusion is clearly false if the statement "Some of our new fleet cars are available for use this month" is true.

- None of our new fleet cars are available for use this month.

Explanation: This conclusion contradicts the meaning of the original statement.

Conclusions for Which There Is Insufficient Information

The two conclusions discussed below are uncertain because the statement "Some of our new fleet cars are available for use this month" does not give us sufficient information to know if they are true or not.

- All of our new fleet cars are available for use this month.

Explanation: This conclusion is uncertain because the original statement "Some of our new fleet cars are available for use this month" refers to just part of the set of new fleet cars. Therefore, strictly speaking, we do not have enough information to draw a conclusion about all of the set. Of course, sometimes we use the initial statement to mean that some -- but not all -- members of one set are members of another set. Therefore, when you interpret a statement about some parts or members of a set, you should be cautious about whether or not the statement is based on knowledge about part of the set or about all of the set. The next uncertain conclusion illustrates the same point.

- Some of our new fleet cars are not available for use this month.

Explanation: This is an uncertain conclusion because saying that there are some new fleet cars that are available for use this month does not itself imply that there are some that are not. For example, someone might have seen several of the new fleet cars being used and might report to you (happily), "Some new cars are available for use!" Jumping to the conclusion that the rest of the cars in the fleet are not available would obviously be mistaken -- in fact, this type of mistake is called an "illogical bias" because it is a common mistake in human reasoning. On the job, these illogical biases can be very costly, at best in terms of monetary cost or, at worst, in terms of human life.

Of course, if you made a statement such as, "I have inspected the records on all the new fleet cars and only some of them are available for use this month," then it would be clear that you know that some of the new cars are unavailable for use.

Self-Test: Section II.A.5. (answers are given on page 114)

In the questions below, you will be given a statement that is followed by four conclusions. Given that the statement is true, you should indicate whether each conclusion is *true* (you can infer the conclusion from the statement) or *false* (you can infer that the conclusion is contrary to the statement), or if there is *insufficient information to decide* whether the conclusion is true or false.

1. Some DHS employees are trained in the use of firearms.

   a. Some people who are trained in the use of firearms are DHS employees. (T / F / I)

   b. All DHS employees are trained in the use of firearms. (T / F / I)

   c. No DHS employees are trained in the use of firearms. (T / F / I)

   d. Some DHS employees are not untrained in the use of firearms. (T / F / I)

2. Some Canadian citizens are eligible to work in the United States.

   a. Some Canadian citizens are ineligible to work in the United States. (T / F / I)

   b. Some Canadian citizens are not ineligible to work in the United States. (T / F / I)

   c. All Canadian citizens are eligible to work in the United States. (T / F / I)

   d. Some people who are eligible to work in the United States are Canadian citizens. (T / F / I)

Section II.A.6.   Conclusions From "Some Are Not" Statements

If you have information that at least some part of a set is excluded from another set, then there is one *true* conclusion you can draw and one conclusion that you know is *false*. There are three other conclusions that are uncertain because you have *insufficient information*.

True Conclusion

The one true conclusion you can draw from the statement "Some of our new fleet cars are not available for use this month" is the following:

- Some of our new fleet cars are unavailable for use this month.

Explanation: This is true because not being available for use this month is synonymous with being unavailable for use this month. If you are interested in studying this form more deeply, you can see that this form is actually a double negation of the original statement.[6] The original statement says:

Some [members of set A] are not [members of set B]

The true conclusion says:

Some [members of set A] are [non-members of set B]

The original verb "are not" was negated and the second set was negated. As you can see, and as you may recall from Section II.A.4, the double negative of the verb canceled itself out and the meaning of the original statement was retained.

False Conclusion

The following statement is false if the initial statement "Some of our new fleet cars are not available for use this month" is true.

- All of our new fleet cars are available for use this month.

Explanation: This conclusion contradicts the information in the initial statement.

Conclusions for Which There Is Insufficient Information

The three conclusions discussed below are all uncertain when an initial statement such as "Some of our new fleet cars are not available for use this month" is true. They are all uncertain because the initial statement only gives us information about some of the new fleet cars.

- None of our new fleet cars is available for use this month.

Explanation: We are not warranted in drawing a conclusion about the entire set of new fleet cars if we only have information about some of them.

- Some vehicles that are available for use this month are not our new fleet cars.

Explanation: This conclusion cannot be legitimately inferred from the initial statement because the initial statement does not give any information about the vehicles that are available for use this month. In fact, the initial statement does not even imply that there *are* vehicles available for use this month.

You might have noticed that the uncertain conclusion above represents the *converse* of the initial statement. That is to say, the order of two sets was exchanged in drawing the

---

[6] **Logic Note.** This form is called the *obverse.*

conclusion. This particular conclusion is another powerful *illogical bias*, another common reasoning mistake that you should try to avoid.

- Some of our new fleet cars are available for use this month.

Explanation: This conclusion is uncertain, given that "Some of our new fleet cars are not available for use this month," because the initial statement has only told us about *some* new fleet cars. It has not said anything about whether any of the rest of the new fleet cars are available for use this month. It does not presume to give information about all of the new fleet cars. This type of conclusion is another illogical bias which you should try to avoid in drawing conclusions from partial information.

If the initial statement had been something like, "I have inspected the records on all of the new fleet cars and only a few are not available for use this month," then you would be justified in concluding that there are some fleet cars that are available for use this month.

Many mistakes based on illogical biases have been made that have ruined budgets or endangered human life. The following example shows this type of mistake: Some areas with rough terrain are not safe to land a helicopter; therefore, some other areas with rough terrain are safe to land a helicopter.

Self-Test: Section II.A.6 (answers are given on page 115)

In the questions below, you will be given a statement that is followed by four conclusions. Given that the statement is true, you should indicate whether each conclusion is *true* (you can infer the conclusion from the statement) or *false* (you can infer that the conclusion is contrary to the statement), or if there is *insufficient information to decide* whether the conclusion is true or false.

1. This morning I received some documents that were not in acceptable form.

    a. This morning, all of the documents I received were in acceptable form. (T / F / I)

    b. This morning I received some documents that were in acceptable form. (T / F / I)

    c. Some documents I received this morning were in unacceptable form. (T / F / I)

    d. None of the documents I received this morning were in acceptable form. (T / F / I)

2. Some computers in our office cannot run this new software.

    a. Some computers that can run this new software are not in our office. (T / F / I)

    b. None of the computers in our office can run this new software. (T / F / I)

    c. Some computers in our office can run this new software. (T / F / I)

    d. All of the computers in our office can run this new software. (T / F / I)

Section II.A.7. Conclusions When the Basic Statements Are False

In the preceding four sections, you have learned about conclusions you can draw when one of the four basic statements is true. However, there are also conclusions you can draw if one of the statements is false. Recognizing these conclusions will further expand your deductive reasoning powers. In this section, you will learn these conclusions for all four of the basic statements.

At first you will find this section easy and you will think it is repetitive relative to the previous section, but as you read the material you will realize inferences from statements that are false can be tricky and that it is very easy to lapse into reasoning errors. Because these inferences occur constantly in real-life situations, it is important that you acquire mastery in handling them.

Conclusions When an "All Are" Statement Is False

A true conclusion. When a statement such as "All of our new fleet cars are available for use this month" is false, the following conclusion must be true.

- Some of our new fleet cars are not available for use this month.

Explanation: You can probably see that if it is not true that all of our new fleet cars are available for use this month, then it must be true that at least some of the cars are not available for use this month.

The following is another example:

> Initial statement: It is not true that all aliens who have proper documents are admissible.

> True conclusion: Some aliens who have proper documents are inadmissible.

Two uncertain conclusions. There are two conclusions that are uncertain when a statement such as "All of our new fleet cars are available for use this month" is known to be false. These two conclusions are:

- None of our new fleet cars are available for use this month.

- Some of our new fleet cars are available for use this month.

Explanation: These conclusions are uncertain because knowing that it is not true that all of our new fleet cars are available for use this month does not give you enough information to conclude that *none* of them are or that *some* of them are.

Conclusions When a "None Are" Statement Is False

A true conclusion. When a statement such as "None of our new fleet cars are available for use this month" is false, then the following conclusion is true:

- Some of our new fleet cars are available for use this month.

Explanation: If it is not true that *none* of the fleet cars are available for use this month, it must be true that *some* of them are available for use this month.

Two uncertain conclusions. The following two conclusions are uncertain if it is not true that none of our new fleet cars are available for use this month:

- All of our new fleet cars are available for use this month.

- Some of our new fleet cars are not available for use this month.

Explanation: These conclusions are uncertain because simply knowing that it is not true that none of the new fleet cars are available for use this month does not give you enough information to know if all of the cars are available for use this month or if some of them are not available for use this month.

Conclusions When a "Some Are" Statement Is False

A true conclusion. When a statement such as "Some of our new fleet cars are available for use this month" is false, then the following conclusion must be true:

- None of our new fleet cars are available for use this month.

Explanation: When we say "it is not true that some of our new fleet cars are available for use this month," we are saying that there are *not* some fleet cars that are available for use this month; in other words there are *no* fleet cars that are available.

The diagrams in Figure 5a and 5b may help to illustrate what we mean when we say that "it is not true that some of our new fleet cars are available for use this month." Figure 5a shows you the meaning of "Some of our new fleet cars are available for use this month." Figure 5b shows that the same statement is false. To indicate this, we have crossed out the semicircle that indicates fleet cars that are available for use this month. This indicates that there are none of our fleet cars in the possible set of vehicles that are available for use this month.

Figure 5a. Diagram for "Some of our new fleet cars are available for use this month."

Figure 5b. Diagram for "It is not true that some of our new fleet cars are available for use this month."

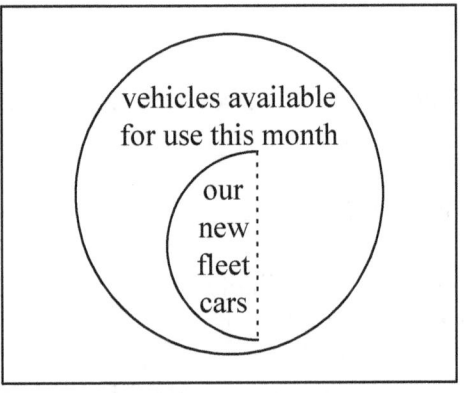
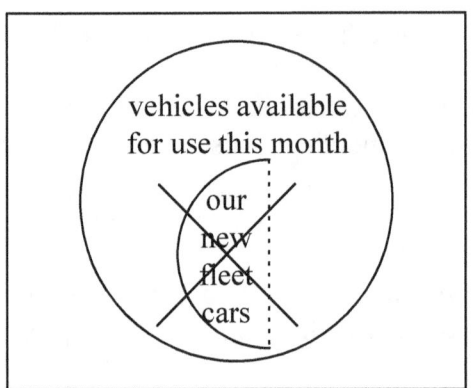

To help you understand the relationship between the falsity of a "Some are" statement and the truth of a "None are" statement, let us look at two more examples.

> Initial statement: It is not true that some of these documents are counterfeit.
> True conclusion: None of these documents are counterfeit.

> Initial statement: It is not true that some of the new computers are laptops.
> True conclusion: None of the new computers are laptops.

Both of the initial statements say that it is not true that some members of the first set are members of the second set. The true conclusion says that therefore no members of the first set are members of the second set.

A false conclusion. The following conclusion is false, when the statement "Some of our new fleet cars are available for use this month" is false:

- All of our new fleet cars are available for use this month.

Explanation: If it is not true that some of the new fleet cars are available for use this month, then it certainly cannot be true that *all* of the cars are available for use this month.

Conclusions When a "Some Are Not" Statement Is False

A true conclusion. When a statement such as "Some of our new fleet cars are not available for use this month" is false, then the following conclusion must be true:

- All of our new fleet cars are available for use this month.

Explanation: When we say "it is not true that some of our new fleet cars are not available for use this month," we mean that there are not *any* fleet cars that are not available for use this month. In other words, we are saying that *all* of our fleet cars are available for use this month. The diagrams in Figure 6a and Figure 6b may help to illustrate what we mean when we say that "it is not true that some of our new fleet cars are not available for use this month." Figure 6a shows you the meaning of "Some of our new fleet cars are not available for use this month." Figure 6b shows that the same statement is false. To indicate this, we have crossed out the semicircle that indicates fleet cars that are not available for use this month. This indicates that there are no fleet cars outside the set of vehicles that are available for use this month.

Figure 6a. Diagram for "Some of our new fleet cars are not available for use this month."

Figure 6b. Diagram for "It is not true that some of our new fleet cars are not available for use this month."

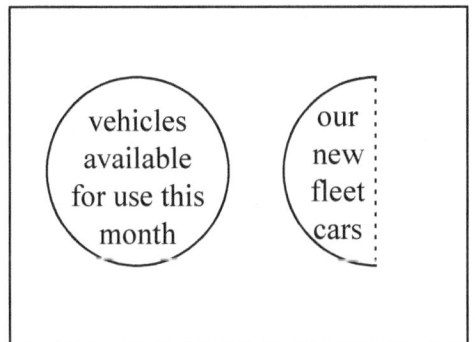
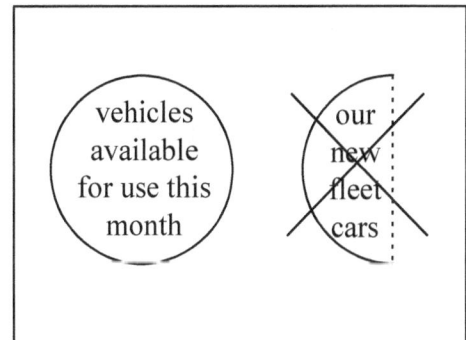

Two more examples are given below to help ensure that you understand the relationship between the falsity of a "Some are not" statement and the truth of an "All are" statement.

Initial statement: It is not true that some of the offices do not have windows.
True conclusion: All of the offices have windows.

Initial statement: It is not true that some employees did not receive the notice.
True conclusion: All employees received the notice.

Both of the initial statements say that it is not true that some members of the first set are *not* members of the second set. The true conclusion says that therefore *all* members of the first set are members of the second set.

28

A false conclusion. The following conclusion is false:

- None of our new fleet cars are available for use this month.

Explanation: If it is not true that some of the new fleet cars are not available for use this month, then it certainly cannot be true that *none* of the cars are available for use this month.

Self-Test: Section II.A.7 (answers are given on page 116)

In the questions below, you will be given a statement that is followed by four conclusions. Given that the statement is false, you should indicate whether each conclusion is *true* (you can infer the conclusion from the statement) or *false* (you can infer that the conclusion is contrary to the statement), or if there is *insufficient information to decide* whether the conclusion is true or false.

1. This statement is false: None of the computers in our office can run the new software.

    a. All of the computers in our office can run the new software. (T / F / I)

    b. Some of the computers in our office can run the new software. (T / F / I)

    c. Some of the computers in our office cannot run the new software. (T / F / I)

2. This statement is false: Some of the employees in our office received awards this year.

    a. All of the employees in our office received awards this year. (T / F / I)

    b. None of the employees in our office received an award this year. (T / F / I)

3. This statement is false: All of the passengers boarding the plane have proper documentation of U.S. citizenship.

    a. None of the passengers boarding the plane have proper documentation of U.S. citizenship. (T / F / I)

    b. Some of the passengers boarding the plane have proper documentation of U.S. citizenship. (T / F / I)

    c. Some of the passengers boarding the plane do not have proper documentation of U.S. citizenship. (T / F / I)

4. This statement is false: Some DHS managers have not completed the new Management Issues training course.

    a. All DHS managers have completed the new Management Issues training course. (T / F / I)

    b. No DHS managers have completed the new Management Issues training course. (T / F / I)

Part II.B. Reasoning with Three Sets

In this part, you will learn about reasoning with three sets by building on what you have already learned about statements that relate two sets. This part, as well as all of Units II and III in this manual, is very important for successful performance in your job. In performing your job, you are frequently called upon to carry out reasoning and decision making relative to three (or more) sets. The study of this part will give you the necessary skills for doing so successfully.

Section II.B.1. Forms for Relating Three Sets

The following example shows how two statements can be used together to draw a new conclusion about the relationship between two sets. You will see in Example 1 that the two statements contain a total of three sets, one of which is contained in both statements. In this and subsequent examples, the statements will be called *premises*. A premise is any evidence that is used to support a conclusion.

> ***Example 1***
> Premise 1:   All recently hired employees are very well qualified.
> Premise 2:   All of our trainees are recently hired employees.
> Conclusion: All of our trainees are very well qualified.

The set that is common to both premises is "recently hired employees." That set can be called the *term of comparison,* although in logic it has traditionally been called the *middle term.*

This reasoning form, which is sometimes called a *syllogism,* allows you to describe the relationship between the set that is found only in the second premise (trainees) and the set that is found only in the first premise (very well qualified [individuals]).

In the example given above, the set "trainees" is completely included in the set "recently hired employees," which itself is completely included in the set "very well qualified [individuals]." Thus, the set "trainees" is completely included in the set "very well qualified [individuals]."

Figure 7 below illustrates the relationships among the sets in Example 1.

Figure 7. Diagram for Example 1.

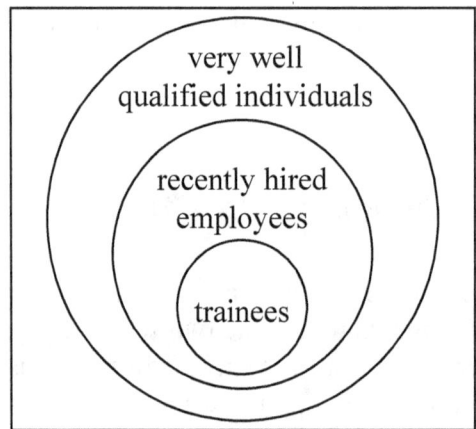

The next example shows you a similar reasoning form which contains a negative premise.

> ***Example 2***
> Premise 1:   No recently hired employee is certified in CPR.
> Premise 2:   All trainees are recently hired employees.
> Conclusion: No trainee is certified in CPR.

In this example, the middle term is once again "recently hired employees." The first statement says that this set is completely excluded from the set of people who are "certified in CPR." Since all trainees are recently hired employees, they are all excluded from the set of people who are certified in CPR. Figure 8 below illustrates the relationships among the three sets in Example 2.

Figure 8. Diagram for Example 2.

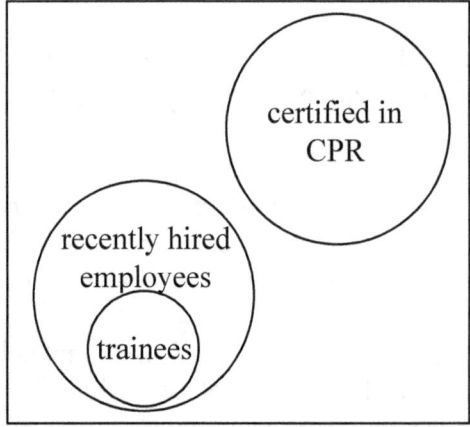

In Examples 1 and 2, the middle term was the subject of the first premise and the predicate term of the second premise. There are three other possible positions for the middle term, and these positions help determine whether or not a conclusion can be reached from the pair of premises. In the next example, the middle term is the predicate term of both premises. You will see that no conclusion can be reached about the relationship between the other two terms.

> ### Example 3
> Premise 1:   All of our analysts are recently hired employees.
> Premise 2:   All of our trainees are recently hired employees.
> Conclusion: No conclusion is possible about the relationship between the sets "trainees" and "analysts."

The first premise says that the set of analysts is completely included in the set of recently hired employees. The second premise says that the set of trainees is also completely included in the set of recently hired employees. However, we have no other information about the set of recently hired employees; it could be very large compared to the other two sets. This leaves open the possibility that all, some, or none of the trainees are analysts.

Figure 9a and 9b below show two possible ways the premises could be represented. The sets of trainees and psychologists might be completely separate, as shown in Figure 9a; or, they might be overlapping, as shown in 9b. Another possibility, not illustrated, is that the two sets overlap completely. We do not have enough information to know which is the correct representation.

Figure 9a. A Possible Representation of Example 3.

Figure 9b. Another Possible Representation of Example 3

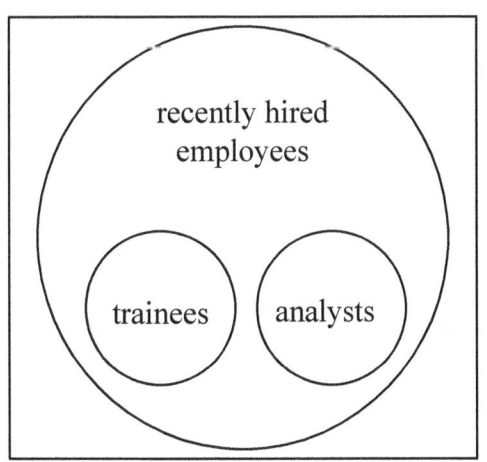

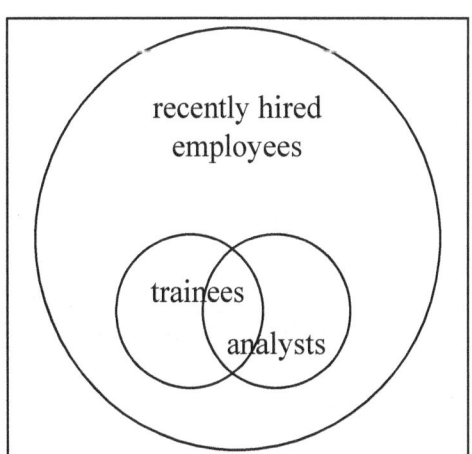

Of all the possible combinations of the basic statements (there are 64 of them), only 15 combinations permit a valid conclusion to be drawn. Therefore, when you come across an example of reasoning in which two sets are compared to a third set, it is important to examine the form of the reasoning very carefully to be sure that the conclusion is valid.

Examples 4, 5, and 6 give you more examples of valid syllogisms.

Example 4

Premise 1:   All agents from this station have been issued the new pistol.
Premise 2:   No one at the firing range today has been issued the new pistol.
Conclusion: No one at the firing range today was an agent from this station.

From the information in Premise 2, we can conclude that no one who has been issued the new pistol was at the firing range today.[7] Since Premise 1 tells us that all agents from this station have been issued the new pistol, we can conclude that no one at the firing range today was an agent from this station. Figure 10 below represents the relationships among the sets in Example 4.

Figure 10. Diagram for Example 4.

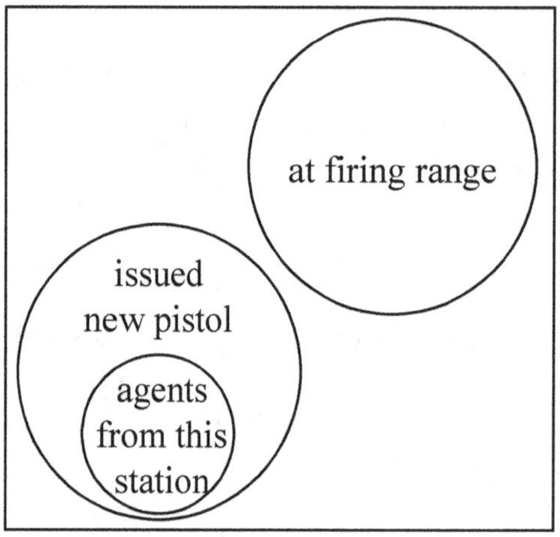

Example 5

Premise 1:   All agents from this station have been issued the new pistol.
Premise 2:   Some agents from this station are new agents.
Conclusion: Some new agents have been issued the new pistol.

From the information in Premise 2, we can conclude that some new agents are agents from this station.[8] Therefore, based on Premise 1, we can conclude that these new agents have

---

[7] **Logic Note**. You may recall from Section II.A.4 that it is valid to exchange the position of the sets in a statement of the form No [members of set A] are [members of set B]. This is called the *converse*.
[8] **Logic Note**. You may recall from Section II.A.5 that it is valid to exchange the position of the sets in a statement of the form Some [members of set A] are [members of set B]. This is again called the *converse*.

been issued new pistols. Figure 11 below represents the relationships among the sets in Example 5.

Figure 11. Diagram for Example 5.

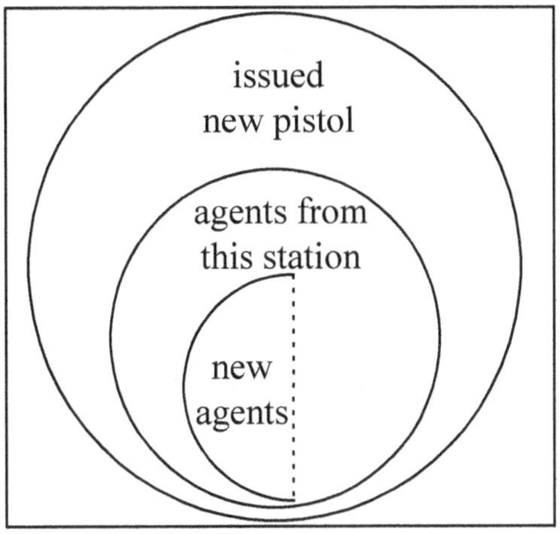

Example 6 is the last example of a syllogism in this section.

> ***Example 6***
> Premise 1:   Some of our trainees are not college graduates.
> <u>Premise 2:   All of our trainees are recently hired employees.</u>
> Conclusion: Some recently hired employees are not college graduates.

From the second premise we can conclude that anyone who is one of our trainees is also one of our recently hired employees. Therefore, when the first premise says that some of our trainees are not college graduates, it is also implying that some of our recently hired employees are not college graduates.

It would be impossible to diagram this syllogism using the type of diagrams that we have been using.[9] If you try to do it, you will find that you run into trouble picturing the set "our trainees," because you have to picture *all* of the set as being included in a second set and *part* of the set as being excluded from a third set.

Why is it useful to know about valid syllogisms?

Valid syllogisms represent useful reasoning forms that enable you to draw new conclusions when you have certain information about three sets. Knowing about syllogisms will help you to build your own arguments and to evaluate the arguments that other people make. As

---

[9] **Logic Note.** There is another type of diagrams, called Venn diagrams, that could be used for this syllogism. These can be found in any Logic book.

we said in the beginning of Part II.B, in real-life job performance you are frequently called upon to carry out reasoning and decision making involving three (or more[10]) sets.

The next section is an optional section that gives you logical rules that you can use to decide whether an argument about three sets is valid or not. In Section II.B.3 you will build on your knowledge by learning to avoid illogical biases in relating three sets.

Self-Test: Section II.B.1 (answers are given on page 117)

For each pair of statements below, underline the middle term and then write a valid conclusion relating the other two terms.

1.   Premise 1: All DHS employees are Federal Government employees.
      Premise 2: All ICE employees are DHS employees.
      Conclusion:

2.   Premise 1: No Canadian citizens are U.S. citizens.
      Premise 2: All citizens of Quebec are Canadian citizens.
      Conclusion:

3.   Premise 1: No District 1 staff has completed the new training.
      Premise 2: All recently hired adjudicators have completed the new training.
      Conclusion:

4.   Premise 1: Some agents are trained in Advanced CPR.
      Premise 2: All employees trained in Advanced CPR passed the Basic CPR course.
      Conclusion:

5.   Premise 1: All ICE vehicles are listed in the vehicle database.
      Premise 2: Some DHS vehicles are not ICE vehicles.
      Conclusion:

---

[10] **Logic Note.** When you have more than three sets, you can make an inference by developing a chain of syllogisms in which the conclusion of the first syllogism would become the first premise of the second. Logicians call this form of reasoning *sorites*.

6.   Premise 1: All persons born in the U.S.A. are U.S. citizens.
       Premise 2: All persons born in the U.S.A. can get social security cards.
       Conclusion:

Section II.B.2. Advanced Topic -- Syllogistic Rules (reading this section is optional)

Applying the rules in this section will allow you to decide quickly whether or not an argument relating three sets permits a valid conclusion. The first three rules are very easy to apply. The fourth and fifth rules require additional explanation, because they introduce the new concept of a *distributed* term.

1.   If both premises are negative, there is no conclusion. (If both premises are negative, the three sets are completely separate and no further conclusion can be drawn.)

2.   If one premise is negative, the conclusion is negative. (If one premise is negative, the essence of the syllogism is to disconnect one set from another through its disconnection from the middle term.)

3.   If neither premise is negative, the conclusion is affirmative. (If both premises are affirmative, there is no reason to conclude anything negative.)

4.   The middle term must be distributed at least once in order for there to be a valid conclusion. (See discussion immediately below.)

5.   No term may be distributed in the conclusion if it is not distributed in the premises. (See discussion immediately below.)

When we say a term is distributed in a premise, we mean that the premise says something about the entire set represented by the term.

- In the statement All [members of set A] are [members of set B], set A is distributed because the statement says that the **entire** set A is included in set B. That is to say, the statement refers to set A in its entirety.

- In the statement No [members of set A] are [members of set B], set A and set B are both distributed because **all** of set A is excluded from **all** of set B.

- In the statement Some [members of set A] are [members of set B], neither term is distributed because we only know about **part** of set A and **part** of set B.

- In the statement Some [members of set A] are not [members of set B], the set B is distributed because the statement says that there are **some** members of set A that are excluded from **all** of set B. (This explanation is a little hard to understand, but it becomes clear when pictured in a diagram. There, the portion of set A is drawn outside the entire set B; hence, it is clearer that we are referring to the whole of set B.)

From the five basic rules, two more very useful rules can be derived:

6.   If both premises refer to only part of a set, there is no conclusion. (It is impossible to relate the parts of the sets that are referred to by the vague quantifier "some.")

7.   If one premise refers to only part of a set, the conclusion refers to only part of a set. (If one premise refers to part of a set, the conclusion cannot generalize legitimately beyond that.)

To gain further appreciation of these rules, we can apply them to some of the syllogisms that have already been presented in Section II.B.1. The syllogism in Example 1 has the following form (with M representing the term that is common to the two premises):

> Premise 1:   All [members of set M] are [members of set B]
> Premise 2:   All [members of set A] are [members of set M]
> Conclusion: All [members of set A] are [members of set B]

This syllogism has two affirmative premises, so the conclusion must be affirmative (rule 3). The middle term M is distributed in the first premise (rule 4). Set A is distributed in the conclusion and in the second premise (rule 5).

Now let us apply the rules to Example 3 in Section II.B.1, which does not have a valid conclusion. This syllogism has the following form:

> Premise 1:   All [members of set B] are [members of set M]
> Premise 2:   All [members of set A] are [members of set M]
> Invalid Conclusions: All [members of set A] are [members of set B]
>   Some [members of set A] are [members of set B]

Since both premises are affirmative, the syllogism would have to have an affirmative conclusion (rule 3). All [members of set A] are [members of set B] and Some [members of set A] are [members of set B] are therefore possible conclusions. However, the middle term M is not distributed in either premise (violation of rule 4). Therefore, the syllogism does not have a valid conclusion.

The Self-Test will give you practice in applying these rules.

Self-Test: Section II.B.2 (answers are given on page 118)

In exercises 1 through 4, indicate which syllogisms are valid. For valid syllogisms, decide which syllogistic rules apply. For invalid syllogisms, decide which syllogistic rules are violated.

1.   Premise 1: All ICE Agents are Department of Homeland Security employees.
        Premise 2: All ICE Agents are Federal Government employees.
        Conclusion: All Federal Government employees are Department of Homeland Security employees.

(valid / invalid)
If valid, which rules apply? If invalid, which rules are violated?

2.   Premise 1: All drug smugglers are violators of anti-drug laws.
<u>Premise 2: No Station 2 detainees are violators of anti-drug laws.</u>
Conclusion: No Station 2 detainees are drug smugglers.
(valid / invalid)
If valid, which rules apply? If invalid, which rules are violated?

3.   Premise 1: Some contraband seized was seized by DHS.
<u>Premise 2: All contraband seized becomes property of the U.S. Government.</u>
Conclusion: Some property of the U.S. Government is contraband seized by the DHS.
(valid / invalid)
If valid, which rules apply? If invalid, which rules are violated?

4.   Premise 1: All illegal immigrants are under the jurisdiction of the DHS.
<u>Premise 2: Some deported persons are illegal immigrants.</u>
Conclusion: Some deported persons are not under the jurisdiction of the DHS.
(valid / invalid)
If valid, which rules apply? If invalid, which rules are violated?

Section II.B.3. Illogical Biases in Relating Three Sets

It has been shown in numerous studies that people make many mistakes when reasoning with three sets. We could say that people have many illogical biases in this type of reasoning. The purpose of this section is to show you the most prevalent of these biases so that you can avoid them yourself.

One of the common mistakes of reasoning is to think that a valid conclusion can be drawn from premises that do not warrant a valid conclusion. For example, in the following two cases no conclusion can be drawn, although people tend to think otherwise.

Premise 1: No biased persons make fair decisions.
<u>Premise 2: No adjudicators are biased.</u>
Invalid Conclusion: No adjudicators make fair decisions.

Premise 1: Some detainees were deported.
<u>Premise 2: Some deported persons came from overseas.</u>
Invalid Conclusion: Some persons who came from overseas were detainees.

If you read the Advanced Topic on syllogistic rules in the previous section, you will see that, in the first example, no conclusion can be drawn because both premises are negative and, in the second example, no conclusion can be drawn because both premises refer only to part of a set. If you construct diagrams for these two forms, you will appreciate graphically the invalidity of these forms. In the first form, the sets are totally disconnected from one another, thus allowing no conclusion. In the second form, the parts of the set denoted by the vague quantifier "some" are undefined and hence cannot be related to one another.

Another common error is to draw a conclusion about an entire set when a conclusion is warranted about only part of a set. The next two examples show this type of error.

> Premise 1: All primary inspections are conducted by one inspector.
> Premise 2: All primary inspections are brief.
> Invalid Conclusion: All brief inspections are conducted by one inspector.
> Valid Conclusion: Some brief inspections are conducted by one inspector.

The first conclusion is invalid because Premise 2 does not give us information about *all* brief inspections. (As you will recall from your study of the converse in Section II.A.3, you cannot conclude that "All brief inspections are primary inspections" from the statement that "All primary inspections are brief.") We can conclude from that premise only that "*some* brief inspections are primary inspections." Therefore, we can only conclude that "some brief inspections are conducted by one inspector."

> Premise 1: No Texans live in Florida.
> Premise 2: All Floridians live in the U.S.A.
> Invalid Conclusion: No persons who live in the U.S.A. are Texan.
> Valid Conclusion: Some persons who live in the U.S.A. are not Texan.

The invalid conclusion to this syllogism is based on the same type of reasoning error that characterized the previous invalid syllogism. From the statement that "All Floridians live in the U.S.A." (Premise 2), you can only conclude that "Some people who live in the U.S.A. are Floridians." Therefore, you can only conclude that "Some people who live in the U.S.A. (the Floridians) are not Texans."

What is the significance of these illogical biases?

These illogical biases serve as a caution to you (and to all of us) to be very careful when drawing conclusions about the relationships among sets. An incorrect conclusion may "feel" right at first and you may be swayed into faulty conclusions that will affect the integrity of your decision making on the job. The antidote to illogical biases is good reasoning: your goal is to become a top reasoner by fine-tuning your skills through the use of this manual.

Self-Test: Section II.B.3 (answers are given on page 119)

For each syllogism below, indicate if the conclusion is valid (true). If the conclusion is not valid (that is, if it is false or if there is insufficient information), determine if there is a different, valid conclusion.

1. Premise 1: No Special Agents failed to qualify with their firearm last week.
    Premise 2. All employees who failed to qualify with their firearm last week must qualify this week.
    Conclusion: No employees who have to qualify with their firearm this week are Special Agents.
    (valid / invalid)
    If applicable, valid conclusion:

2. Premise 1: All requests for computer assistance must be made to the Help Desk.
    Premise 2: All Help Desk requests are entered into the service system.
    Conclusion: All entries into the service system are requests for computer assistance.
    (valid / invalid)
    If applicable, valid conclusion:

3. Premise 1: All furniture in the ABC building is the property of DHS.
    Premise 2: Some of this department's furniture is in the ABC building.
    Conclusion: Some of this department's furniture is the property of DHS.
    (valid / invalid)
    If applicable, valid conclusion:

4. Premise 1: Some space on this floor belongs to the Logistics office.
    Premise 2: Some space of the Logistics office is assigned to Jim.
    Conclusion: Some space assigned to Jim is on this floor.
    (valid / invalid)
    If applicable, valid conclusion:

Part II.C. Reasoning with Connectives

Reasoning with connectives is something that you do everyday. For example, when you use a sentence such as "If it rains tomorrow, then I will not wash the car," you are using a connective sentence called the *conditional*. Similarly, the statement "People who are eligible for this job have a college degree or three years of responsible experience" is a connective sentence called an *alternation*.

Connectives are words such as "and," "either...or," and "if...then" that express relationships between simple statements. These simple statements express possible or actual circumstances such as "it rains tomorrow," "I will not wash the car," and "you have a college degree."

The Federal Government workplace, including the law enforcement professions, requires employees to reason with connectives constantly. Frequently, these connectives are used in very complex combinations, such as those found in laws pertaining to immigration and naturalization.

The purpose of this part of the training is to make you aware of the connectives that you use everyday and of what their implications are. This training should ensure that you use connectives correctly in your reasoning, especially when you are dealing with complex relationships. It will help you appreciate when work situations express a relationship embodied in one of the connectives, such as an "if...then" situation or an "either...or" situation. A good knowledge of connectives will help you formulate problems and decisions correctly so that you can anticipate the consequences of your choices and actions in the performance of your job.

We will begin by talking about the simple connective called *conjunction* and then return to the subject of negation, which we first discussed with reference to reasoning with two sets.

Section II.C.1. Conjunction and Negation

Conjunction

Conjunction conveys the meaning of the English word "and"; it says that two or more things occur together. The following sentences contain conjunctions:

- Everyday I open the safe in the morning and she locks it at close of business.

- You will receive on-the-job training in addition to classroom training.

- The Attorney General and the Commissioner will attend the ceremony.

Notice that in the second and third examples, the conjunction joins two nouns (for example, on-the-job training and classroom training) rather than two simple statements. Implicitly, however, both of these sentences contain two simple sentences. For example, the second sentence could be rewritten (somewhat inefficiently) as:

- You will receive on-the-job training and you will receive classroom training.

The third sentence could be rewritten as:

- The Attorney General will attend the ceremony and the Commissioner will attend the ceremony.

It should be mentioned here that a conjunction can be used in the same sentence with another connective to make a more complex sentence, such as the following:

- If you complete both classroom training and on-the-job training, then you will have completed the basic requirements.

Notation for connectives. In order to help in the rest of our discussion, we will introduce some notation from the logic of connectives. In formal logic, simple statements are represented by lower-case letters, such as p, q, and r. These letters represent the statements that are joined together by connectives. The following table shows how some of our earlier examples of conjunctions can be represented.

Connective	Statement	Connective	Statement
	I open the safe in the morning	and	she locks the safe at close of business
	p		Q
	The Attorney General will attend the ceremony	and	the Commissioner will attend the ceremony
	p		Q
If	you complete classroom training and* you complete on-the-job training	then	you will have completed the basic requirements
If	p and* q		R

*Note: The word "and" is an embedded connective; that is to say, it is embedded within the primary connective "if...then."

Negation

The correct use of negation is an essential part of reasoning with connectives. You can negate a simple statement or a complex statement that contains connectives. In all cases, the negation means "It is not true that" or "It is not the case that." Negating a sentence simply denies what the sentence says.

The following three examples show you how negation is used with sentences of different levels of complexity. The examples also show how the notation is used.

- *Negate a simple sentence*: It is not true that I open the safe in the morning.   not p

- *Negate a conjunction*: It is not the case that both the Attorney General and the Commissioner will attend the ceremony.   not (p and q)

- *Negate a complex connective sentence*: It is not true that if you complete classroom training and on-the-job training, you will have finished the training program.
  not (if p and q, then r)

Self-Test: Section II.C.1 (answers are given on page 119)

1. Which of the following sentences expresses a conjunction? For those that express a conjunction, underline the phrases or statements that are joined.

   a. The Department of Homeland Security both confers benefits and enforces laws.
      (conjunction / not a conjunction)

   b. Aliens can enter the U. S. as either immigrants or nonimmigrants.
      (conjunction / not a conjunction)

   c. To be successful, a teletraining instructor must maintain "eye contact" with the viewers and must involve viewers in interactive exercises.
      (conjunction / not a conjunction)

   d. A complete computer set-up includes a processor, a display, a keyboard, and a mouse.
      (conjunction / not a conjunction)

   e. If the annual fire drill is conducted tomorrow, our conference will be interrupted.
      (conjunction / not a conjunction)

2. Write the negation of each of the following sentences in the space provided below.

   a. The new vehicles have four-wheel drive.

   b. Agents López and Johnson are on annual leave today.

   c. The agency will use both classroom training and computer-based training in the future.

   d. Either you or I will attend the meeting.

   e. If it rains, the ceremony will be canceled.

Section II.C.2. The Conditional

The *conditional* is the most important type of connective sentence. It represents circumstances that are found everywhere in life. In fact, if after studying this section you take a look around your home or office, you will find many implicit and explicit examples of the conditional.

A conditional sentence has the form "If p then q." Two examples of conditional sentences are:

- If you are an employee of DHS, then you are a Federal employee.

- If there is a credible bomb threat to an office building, then the building is evacuated until a search is completed.

In the first sentence, the statement "you are an employee of DHS" would be represented by the letter p, and the statement "you are a Federal employee" would be represented by the letter q. In the second sentence, the statement "there is a credible bomb threat to an office building" would be represented by p and "the building is evacuated until a search is completed" would be represented by q.

In a conditional sentence, the first simple statement (the one represented by p) is known as the *antecedent*. The second simple statement (represented by q) is known as the *consequent*. (The table below shows the parts of a conditional sentence.) The conditional sentence says that if the antecedent is true, then the consequent must also be true. Another way of expressing this is to say that the antecedent cannot be true if the consequent is false.

The parts of a conditional sentence

Antecedent	Consequent
[If] you are an employee of DHS,	[then] you are a Federal employee.
[If] there is a credible bomb threat to an office building,	[then] the building is evacuated until a search is completed.

To understand the meaning of the conditional, it may help to consider some examples based on the conditional sentence "If you are an employee of DHS, then you are a Federal employee."

- Suppose we had the information that "Pat is an employee of DHS." Taking that information into account with the conditional, we could conclude that "Pat is a Federal employee." (Symbolic version: If p then q; p is true, therefore q is true.) The entire formula is:

> If you are an employee of DHS, then you are a Federal employee.
> <u>Pat is an employee of DHS.</u>
> Therefore, Pat is a Federal employee.

- Suppose we had the information that "Lee is not a Federal employee." Taking that information into account with the conditional, we would be able to conclude that "Lee is not an DHS employee." (Symbolic version: If p then q; q is not true, therefore p is not true.) The formula is:

> If you are an employee of DHS, then you are a Federal employee.
> <u>Lee is not a Federal employee.</u>
> Therefore, Lee is not an employee of DHS.

There are two conclusions that **cannot** be drawn on the basis of the conditional. First, if the antecedent is false, you cannot draw a conclusion about whether or not the consequent is false. The reason is that the range covered by the consequent is potentially larger than the range covered by the antecedent. The following example should show why this is the case.

- Suppose we had the information that "Adrian is not an employee of DHS." We would not be able to conclude that "Adrian is not a Federal employee," because Adrian might work for another Federal agency. We really cannot tell whether or not Adrian is a Federal employee based on the information we have. (Symbolic version: If p then q; p is false, therefore, q may be either true or false.) The formula is:

> If you are an employee of DHS, then you are a Federal employee.
> <u>Adrian is not an employee of DHS.</u>
> Invalid conclusion: Adrian is not a Federal employee.

The second case in which you cannot draw a conclusion from the conditional occurs if you know that the consequent is true. From that information, you cannot tell if the antecedent is true or not. Once again, the reason is that the range covered by the consequent is potentially larger than the range covered by antecedent. The following example illustrates this point.

- Suppose we had information that "René is a Federal employee." We would not be able to conclude that "René is an employee of DHS," because René might work for another Federal agency. We really cannot tell whether or not René is a DHS employee based on the information we have. (Symbolic version: If p then q; q is true, therefore p may be either true or false.) The formula is:

> If you are an employee of DHS, then you are a Federal employee.
> <u>René is a Federal employee.</u>
> Invalid Conclusion: René is an employee of DHS.

45

The following chart summarizes conclusions that can and cannot be made from the conditional sentence "If you are an employee of DHS, then you are a Federal employee" (If p then q).

Initial conditional sentence: "If you are an employee of DHS, then you are a Federal employee." (If p then q)

Conclusion	Validity
If you are not a Federal employee, then you are not an employee of DHS. (If not q, then not p)[11]	valid
If you are a Federal employee, then you are an employee of DHS. (If q, then p)	invalid
If you are not an employee of DHS, then you are not a Federal employee. (If not p, then not q)	invalid

The second conclusion in the table is called the *converse*. The converse is created by interchanging the two parts of the sentence, the antecedent and the consequent. As you may recall from Section II.A.3, this form is not a valid conclusion from a statement such as "All [members of set A] are [members of set B]." It is also not a valid conclusion from a conditional sentence.

The third conclusion in the table is called the *inverse*. The inverse is created by negating both terms, but leaving them in their original positions. Like the converse, the inverse is not valid because it is not equivalent in meaning to the original conditional sentence "If you are an employee of DHS, then you are a Federal employee."

The inverse and converse of the conditional are both powerful **illogical biases**. They represent erroneous conclusions that people tend to make frequently. You should study them carefully to be sure that you can avoid making these erroneous conclusions yourself.

In the examples that we provided on the previous page it was easy to see why the inverse and the converse were wrong, because you are well aware of the relationship between being a DHS employee and being a Federal employee. In order to study the biases further, let us see how they work with the second conditional sentence: "If there is a credible bomb threat to a Federal office building, then the building is evacuated until a search is completed." Assuming this sentence is true, let us look at what conclusions we can and cannot draw when the four types of evidence are presented.

---

[11] **Logic Note**. This logical form, in which the two parts of the sentence exchange position and are negated is called the contrapositive. The contrapositive was first introduced in Section II.A.3.

Second conditional sentence: "If there is a credible bomb threat to a Federal office building, then the building is evacuated until a search is completed."

Conclusion	Validity
If we know that there is a credible bomb threat to a particular Federal office building, we can conclude that the building is evacuated until a search is completed. (If p, then q)	valid
If we know that a particular Federal office building has not been evacuated pending a search, then we can conclude that there has not been a credible bomb threat to that building. (If not-q, then not-p)	valid
If we know that there has not been a credible bomb threat to a particular Federal office building, we cannot conclude that the building has not been evacuated pending a search, because it may have been evacuated for some other reason (a fire alarm, for example). (If not-p, then not-q cannot be concluded)	invalid
If we know that a particular building has been evacuated pending a search, we cannot conclude that there has been a credible bomb threat to that building, because, once again, there may have been some other reason for the evacuation. (If q, then p cannot be concluded)	invalid

It is recommended that you study the above examples and the exercises in the Self-Test so that you can detect illogical biases in the conditional and avoid making these erroneous conclusions.

Other Ways of Expressing the Conditional

The conditional is sometimes expressed without using the connective words "if...then." Some of these alternative expressions are "when," "whenever," "any time that." For example, the sentence about bomb threats could have be written in the following way:

- "Whenever there is a credible bomb threat to a Federal office building, that building is always evacuated until a search is completed." This sentence contains the basic idea of the conditional: If p occurs, then q occurs.

Another way of expressing the conditional is to use the connective words "only if." However, the expression "only if" represents conditionality opposite to that which might initially appear to be the case. For example, in the sentence "You are an employee of DHS only if you are a Federal employee," the antecedent of the conditional is the first part of the sentence ("You are an employee of DHS"), rather than the second part. The sentence means exactly the same thing as the sentence we used as our original example of the conditional: "If you are an employee of DHS, then you are a Federal employee."

The conditional is also often expressed by using the word "if," but leaving the word "then" as understood but not expressed. For example, you could say "If you are an employee of DHS, you are a Federal employee."

Self-Test: Section II.C.2 (answers are given on page 120)

1. Which of the following sentences expresses a conditional? For each conditional sentence, underline the antecedent and the consequent.

   a. If you contribute to the Combined Federal Campaign through payroll deduction, then there is a record of a deduction on your biweekly earnings statement. (conditional / not a conditional)

   b. If an international flight arrives, Inspectors process the arriving passengers. (conditional / not a conditional)

   c. You can take the advanced supervisory course only if you have taken the basic supervisory course. (conditional / not a conditional)

   d. I will either attend computer training or use the computerized tutorial or both. (conditional / not a conditional)

   e. Whenever an entire office undergoes a move, there is an inevitable period of disruption. (conditional / not a conditional)

2. Each of the following items contains a pair of statements that might be joined in a conditional sentence. Write a conditional sentence based on each pair in the space provided below.

   Example: a person is French, a person is European
          If you are French, then you are European.

   a. a person is a CBP Inspector, a person works for DHS

   b. a person is hired into the Border Patrol, a person attends training in Glynco

   c. a person receives e-mail messages, a person's computer is connected to a network

   d. a person studies a foreign language enthusiastically, a person develops a good vocabulary in a foreign language

In questions 3 and 4 below, you will be given a conditional statement that is followed by four conclusions. Given that the statement is true, you should indicate whether each conclusion is *true* (you can infer the conclusion from the statement) or *false* (you can infer that the conclusion is contrary to the statement), or if there is *insufficient information to decide* whether the conclusion is true or false.

3. Conditional sentence: If the computer was purchased for someone on our team, the A-team, then it has modem.

    a. The computer used by Mary has a modem; therefore, it was purchased for the A-team. (T / F / I)

    b. John uses one of the computers that was purchased for the A-team; therefore, it has a modem. (T / F / I)

    c. The computer used by Tom does not have a modem; therefore, it was not originally purchased for the A-team. (T / F / I)

    d. The computer used by Anne was purchased for the B-team originally; therefore, it does not have a modem. (T / F / I)

4. Conditional sentence: If we request the same spending level as last year, our budget will be approved.

    a. We requested a higher spending level than last year; therefore, our budget will not be approved. (T / F / I)

    b. Our budget was not approved; therefore, we did not request the same spending level as last year. (T / F / I)

    c. We requested the same spending level as last year; therefore, our budget will not be approved. (T / F / I)

    d. We requested the same spending level as last year; therefore, our budget will be approved. (T / F / I)

Section II.C.3. Other Basic Connectives

This section presents three other basic connectives -- biconditionality, the alternation, and the disjunction. You will find that these forms represent situations that you find in your everyday experience.

49

Biconditionality

A *biconditional* sentence expresses conditionality that goes, in a manner of speaking, in two directions. The following sentence expresses biconditionality:

> If the Secretary of DHS is the director of your agency, then you are an employee of DHS; and if you are an employee of DHS, then the Secretary of DHS is the director of your agency.

A simpler way of expressing the idea in this sentence is to say: "The Secretary of DHS is the director of your agency if and only if you are an employee of DHS."

A symbolic expression of the biconditional sentence is: If p then q, and if q then p. Another way of expressing the biconditional is to say "p if and only if q."

The following chart summarizes all of the conclusions that can be made from this biconditional sentence.

Initial biconditional sentence: The Secretary of DHS is the director of your agency if and only if you are an employee of DHS (p if and only if q)

Conclusion	Validity
If you are not an employee of DHS, the Secretary of DHS is not the director of your agency.[12] (If not q, then not p)	valid
If you are an employee of DHS, the Secretary of DHS is the director of your agency. (If q, then p)	valid
If the Secretary of DHS is not the director of your agency, then you are not an employee of DHS. (If not p, then not q)	valid

The second conclusion in the table is called the *converse*, because the parts of the sentence are interchanged. The third conclusion is called the *inverse*, because both parts of the sentence are negated.

You can see that all of the conclusions are valid, in contrast to the case with the conditional. As a consequence, there are no illogical biases for reasoning with the biconditional. The reason why this occurs is *not* because the inverse and the converse have all of a sudden

---

[12] **Logic Note**. This logical form, in which the two parts of the sentence exchange positions and are negated is called the *contrapositive*. The contrapositive was first introduced in Section II.A.3 and was then reintroduced in the discussion of the conditional in Section II.C.2.

become logically valid. The reason is that both statements refer to exactly the same individuals or things (in other words, p is the same as q). Accordingly, if one statement is true, the other is also true, and if one statement is false the other is also false.

Alternation

A sentence that is an *alternation* says: Either p or q, or both p and q. An example of an alternation is:

- This malfunctioning computer has either a damaged hard drive or too little memory, or both of these problems.

The alternants are the simple statements that may be true or false. If the alternation is true and if it is discovered that one of the alternants is false, then the other alternant must be true. For example, if the sentence about the malfunctioning computer is true and it is discovered that the computer does not have too little memory, then we would have to conclude that the computer's hard drive is damaged.

Another example of an alternation is the following:

- This report must have been written either by Robert or by Clara or by the two of them together.

If you find out that Clara did not write the report, then you can conclude that Robert did.

Disjunction

A *disjunction* is a sentence that has the following form: Not both p and q. You can see that this is the negation of the conjunction of p and q. It states that "It is not the case that both p and q are true." A real-life example of a disjunction would be:

- An employee cannot take both annual leave and sick leave at the same time.

The disjuncts are the basic statements that cannot both be true together. If one of the disjuncts is known to be true, the other one must be false. For example, if we knew that a certain employee had taken eight hours of annual leave yesterday, we would have to conclude that the same employee did not take sick leave yesterday.

Another example of a disjunction is:

- An alien cannot be both deported and returned voluntarily to the country of origin.

If you learn that a certain alien returned voluntarily to his or her country of origin, then you know that the alien was not deported.

Self-Test: Section II.C.3 (answers are given on page 122)

1. Decide if each of the following sentences is a conditional, biconditional, alternation, or disjunction.

   a. If the suspect's file was filed in the right place, it is filed under "S."
      (conditional / biconditional / alternation / disjunction)

   b. The Chief's office will hold a sofa and chair or a small conference table and chairs, but not both. (conditional / biconditional / alternation / disjunction)

   c. Your computer can be linked to the printer in Room 243, the printer in Room 246, or both. (conditional / biconditional / alternation / disjunction)

   d. If and only if you work more than eight hours in one day are you eligible for overtime. (conditional / biconditional / alternation / disjunction)

   e. If the evidence is strong enough for probable cause then it is strong enough for reasonable suspicion. (conditional / biconditional / alternation / disjunction)

In questions 2 and 3 below, you will be given a statement that is followed by four conclusions. Given that the statement is true, you should indicate whether each conclusion is *true* (you can infer the conclusion from the statement) or *false* (you can infer that the conclusion is contrary to the statement), or if there is *insufficient information to decide* whether the conclusion is true or false.

2. Statement: The Jeep either has a faulty starter, bad spark plugs, or both.

   a. The Jeep has a faulty starter; therefore, the Jeep does not have bad spark plugs.
      (T / F / I)

   b. The Jeep has bad spark plugs; therefore, the Jeep has a faulty starter.
      (T / F / I)

   c. The Jeep does not have bad spark plugs; therefore, the Jeep has a faulty starter.
      (T / F / I)

   d. The Jeep does not have a faulty starter; therefore, the Jeep has bad spark plugs.
      (T / F / I)

3. Statement: No branch in this office has both a color printer and a black-and-white printer.

   a. A branch has a color printer; therefore, the branch does not have a black-and-white printer. (T / F / I)

   b. A branch does not have a black-and-white printer; therefore, the branch does not have a color printer. (T / F / I)

   c. A branch does not have a black-and-white printer; therefore, the branch has a color printer. (T / F / I)

   d. A branch has a black-and-white printer; therefore, the branch has a color printer. (T / F / I)

Section II.C.4. Advanced Topic -- Complex Connectives

Although this is an advanced topic, it is extremely important in real-life reasoning performance. You are strongly advised to study it when you have time to concentrate on it and to give it the attention it deserves.

The complex connectives we will present fall into two categories: extended forms and compound forms. We will present these separately.

Extended Forms

The extended forms we will present are based on the conditional. The forms each have two conditional premises. The first form is based on two straightforward conditionals as in the following example:

> Premise 1: If additional staff are assigned, special funding will be needed.
> Premise 2: If it is a holiday weekend, additional staff are assigned.
> Conclusion: Therefore, if it is a holiday weekend, special funding will be needed.

You can see that the same statement ("additional staff are assigned") is the consequent of the second premise and the antecedent of the first premise. It is similar to the middle term in the logic of three sets (see Section II.B.1). This same formula can be represented in symbols in the following way:

> If q then r
> If p then q
> Therefore, If p then r

The next extended form involves negation. An example of this form is as follows:

Premise 1: If Group B had the surveillance equipment, then Group C could not have watched the compound last night.
<u>Premise 2: If Group C had the Team Truck, then Group C watched the compound last night.</u>
Conclusion: Therefore, if Group C had the Team Truck, then Group B did not have the surveillance equipment.

To understand why this conclusion is valid, start by looking at the second premise. The consequent of that premise, "Group C watched the compound last night," is equivalent to the negation (or the contradiction) of the consequent of the first premise, "Group C could not have watched the compound last night." When we negate the consequent, we must also negate the antecedent, "Group B had the surveillance equipment." (Refer to the discussion and table on valid conclusions from the conditional in Section II.C.2.) Therefore, if we know that Group C had the Team Truck, then we must conclude that Group B did not have the surveillance equipment.

The symbolic version of this formula is as follows:

> If r then not q
> <u>If p then q</u>
> Therefore, If p then not r

Compound Forms

This is the last set of deductive forms to be presented. These last forms are just a sample of the many ways in which the various connectives can be combined to produce more complex forms. Therefore, as you study these forms, you should be learning the basic principles for combining forms rather than trying to memorize any specific ones.

You have already seen in Section II.C.1 that a conjunction can be used as the antecedent in a conditional (If p and q, then r). This form demonstrates the principle that a basic connective form can be used as one of the terms in another basic form. Some other examples would be the following:

- alternation as antecedent of conditional: If either John or Mary conducts the meeting, the meeting will be a success.
- disjunction as consequent of conditional: If we do not receive additional funds, we cannot both hire more staff and buy more equipment.
- alternation as one of two conjuncts: Both the Assistant Chief and either Agent Jones or Agent Preston (or both) must attend.

These forms are presented in symbols as follows:

- alternation as antecedent of conditional: If either p or q, then r
- disjunction as consequent of conditional: If p, then not both q and r
- alternation as one of two conjuncts: Both p and either q or r (or both q and r)

54

The second principle for using these compound forms is that the basic form that is embedded must be treated as a single unit. If the unit is negated, the entire embedded basic form must be negated. The following examples show how this principle is applied to the compound forms presented. We will show the valid conclusion in which the antecedent and consequent are exchanged and negated.[13]

Statement 1: If either John or Mary conducts the meeting, the meeting will be a success.

<u>Valid conclusion:</u>
If the meeting is not a success, then neither John nor Mary conducted it.

Statement 2: If the new information system is implemented, electronic records cannot have both restricted and unrestricted access.

<u>Valid conclusion:</u>
If electronic records have both restricted and unrestricted access, the new information system has not been implemented.

The symbolic version of these forms is as follows:

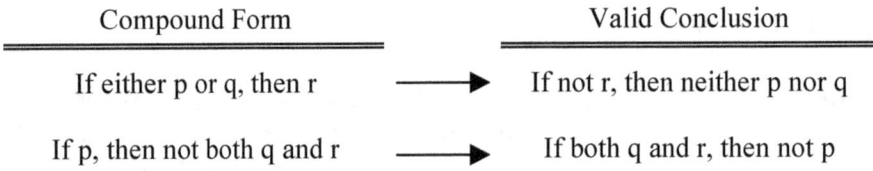

Compound Form	Valid Conclusion
If either p or q, then r	If not r, then neither p nor q
If p, then not both q and r	If both q and r, then not p

Illogical Biases with Extended and Compound Forms

Any extended or compound form that is based on the conditional will be subject to the same illogical biases as the conditional. These two biases are, you will recall, the inverse and the converse.

The illogical biases for the *extended conditional* are shown using our previous example:

Premise 1: If additional staff are assigned, special funding will be needed.
<u>Premise 2: If it is a holiday weekend, additional staff are assigned.</u>
Valid conclusion: Therefore, if it is a holiday weekend, special funding will be needed.

* Inverse (invalid): Therefore, if it is not a holiday weekend, special funding will not be needed.

* Converse (invalid): Therefore, if special funding is needed, it is a holiday weekend.

---

[13] You may recall that this form is called the *contrapositive*.

The illogical biases for the *compound conditional* are shown using our previous example:

> Premise: If either John or Mary conducts the meeting, the meeting will be a success.

* Inverse (invalid): If neither John nor Mary conducts the meeting, the meeting will not be a success.

* Converse (invalid): If the meeting is a success, then either John or Mary conducted it.

Guarding against illogical biases is probably more difficult in these more complex forms than it is for the simple conditional form. Consequently, one should use even greater vigilance to avoid these biases.

Self-Test: Section II.C.4 (answers are given on page 123)

You will be given a statement that is followed by five conclusions. Given that the statement is true, you should indicate whether each conclusion is *true* (you can infer the conclusion from the statement) or *false* (you can infer that the conclusion is contrary to the statement), or if there is *insufficient information to decide* whether the conclusion is true or false.

Statement: If the consultant's recommendations are implemented, we will increase efficiency by 15% and reduce costs by 10%.

1. Efficiency increased by 15% and costs were reduced by 10%; therefore, the consultant's recommendations were implemented. (T / F / I)

2. Efficiency increased by 15% but costs were unchanged; therefore, the consultant's recommendations were not implemented. (T / F / I)

3. The consultant's recommendations were implemented; therefore, efficiency increased by 15% and costs were reduced by 10%. (T / F / I)

4. Costs were reduced by 10%; therefore, the consultant's recommendations were implemented. (T / F / I)

5. The plan to be implemented will either increase efficiency by 15% or reduce costs by 10% but not both; therefore, the consultant's recommendations are not implemented by this plan. (T / F / I)

Part II.D. Using Language Correctly in Deduction

You have finished studying the basic forms for correct deductive reasoning. Perhaps you have noticed in studying these forms that if your language is not compatible with these forms, then conclusions that appear to be deductively correct will actually be incorrect.

It is important to avoid ambiguity in language at all times, but especially when using deductive forms. When you use a word to represent a set of things, you should be sure that you do not change definitions from one use of the word to another. The following example of reasoning with three sets shows the problem created by using an ambiguous term.

> All newly hired employees should be briefed on Federal employee benefits.
> Some newly hired employees were RIFed from other Federal agencies.
>
> Therefore, some employees who were RIFed from other Federal agencies should be briefed on Federal employee benefits.

In this syllogism, the middle term -- newly hired employees -- refers to different sets in the two premises. In the first premise, it clearly refers to employees who are new to Federal Government employment. In the second premise, the term also includes employees who have worked for another Federal agency before, but who have recently been hired by this agency. Since the middle term has two different meanings, it obviously cannot serve as the term of comparison for the other two terms. Thus, the syllogism is not valid.

The above example is instructive because it illustrates a common cause of ambiguity -- mistaking part of a set for the whole. The term "newly hired employees" in the first premise refers to a subset of the set referred to in the second premise. In the second premise, "newly hired employees" refers to all employees who are new to the agency, while in the first premise the term refers to only those new employees who are new to the Federal service.

Another common problem encountered in using language to represent logical forms is the use of incorrect negations. That is, two words may be used as the negation of each other when in fact they are not. For example, the words "hot" and "cold" represent opposite ends of a continuum, but they do not represent the negation of each other. Something could be non-hot and yet not be cold. Thus, the negation of "hot" must be "not hot" rather than "cold."

Unit III. Induction 1 -- Reasoning About Real-World Events

Part III.A. Introduction to Inductive Reasoning

Inductive reasoning, as you learned in Unit I, is reasoning that occurs in the absence of complete information. Induction leads to conclusions that are not **necessarily** true but only have some probability of being true. In inductive reasoning, the evidence does not guarantee the truth of the conclusion, but it does give us a good reason to believe in the truth of the conclusion. We can only say that the premises confirm or support the conclusion. This is in contrast to deductive reasoning, in which the truth of the evidence makes the truth of the conclusion certain.

Why Learn About Induction?

Induction is important in all human activity, from the ordinary activities of daily life through the highest levels of scientific inquiry. Induction is the type of reasoning we use to draw conclusions about the real world. We use induction to form generalizations, to make predictions, and to develop explanations. It is a key component in problem solving and decision making. Thus, induction is an essential job-related thinking skill.

Comparison of Deductive and Inductive Forms

Let us look at and compare some deductive conclusions with apparently similar inductive conclusions. The table below shows the premises and conclusions for deductive and inductive forms. The explanation after the table will guide you in understanding the similarities and differences.

	Deductive	**Inductive**
Premise(s)	Of all first-line supervisors in the agency, 95% have taken the basic supervisory course.	Of all first-line supervisors in the agency, 95% have taken the basic supervisory course. Pat is one of 20 first-line supervisors in Sector X.
Conclusions	Nearly all first-line supervisors in the agency have taken the basic supervisory course. Some people who have taken the basic supervisory course are first-line supervisors in the agency.	It is very likely that Pat has taken the basic supervisory course. Probably some of the people who have taken the basic supervisory course are first-line supervisors from Sector X.

The first premise is the same for both the deductive and inductive columns. It is a statement that relates the two sets of "first-line supervisors in the agency" and "people who have taken the basic supervisory course." It states that 95% of first-line supervisors in the agency have taken the course. You can see that this statement is not quite a universal statement, but it has more information than a statement using the vague quantifier "some."

We have drawn two deductive conclusions from this premise. In saying that "Nearly all first-line supervisors in the agency have taken the basic supervisory course," we are simply replacing the quantity "95%" with the expression "nearly all." Assuming that 95% meets our definition of "nearly all," we are essentially restating the same information as the original premise. The second conclusion, "Some people who have taken the basic course in supervisory skills are first-line supervisors in the agency," is a valid conclusion from the statement "Of all first-line supervisors in the agency, 95% have taken the basic supervisory course." (See Section II.A.5.) Clearly, these conclusions are deductive; that is, they must be true if the premise is true.

In the inductive column we have added a premise about an individual: "Pat is one of 20 first-line supervisors in Sector X." Then, we have drawn two conclusions that are inductive. The first says that it is very likely that Pat has taken the basic supervisory course. This conclusion meets our criteria for inductive reasoning. First, it is based on incomplete information. We do not have enough information to know for sure that Pat has taken the course. Second, the conclusion is not true with certainty. Pat may be among the 5% of first-line supervisors in the agency who did not attend the training. However, given our evidence that nearly all first-line supervisors did attend, it is very probable that Pat attended. Thus, the conclusion has a high degree of probability (but not absolute certainty) associated with it.

Criteria for Correct Induction

There are criteria for correct induction. First and foremost among these is the requirement that the degree of probability claimed for the conclusion must be supported by the premises. In our example involving the supervisor Pat, the conclusion that she is "very likely to have taken the basic supervisory course" is clearly supported by the information that 95% of first-level supervisors in the agency have taken it. If we had concluded that she had certainly taken the course or that she probably had not taken the course, our conclusion would not have been supported by the evidence.

The second requirement is the requirement for use of the *total available evidence*. This means that when forming an inductive conclusion, you should use all the evidence available to you that is relevant to the conclusion. You may have a great deal of information that is relevant or very little. Regardless of how much information you have, your inductive reasoning is considered correct if you take all relevant information that you know into account. You may need to revise your conclusion later if you obtain additional information that casts doubt on the correctness of your original conclusion.

In the example given earlier about Pat, the first-level supervisor from Sector X, it is possible that you might obtain the additional information that "Supervisors in Sector X have attended the basic supervisory course in lower-than-average proportions, because of other urgent initiatives in the last year." Then, you would not be justified in concluding that there was a 95% chance that Pat had attended the training, because you would be ignoring a relevant piece of information. You would be justified in concluding that there was less than a 95% chance that Pat had attended the training.

The Meaning of Probability

We have been using the concept of probability to represent the likelihood that a conclusion is true, given certain evidence. Another way of expressing this is to say that probability represents the *degree of confirmation* for the conclusion provided by the premises. This is the common interpretation of probability in inductive logic.

Probabilities vary from 0 to 1. The value of 1 represents absolute confirmation -- a condition that applies only to deductive conclusions. A value of 0 represents no confirmation. For the range between 0 and 1, numerical values may or may not be assigned. Various words are used to refer to the degrees of certainty within this range. For example, a typical meaning for the word "probably" is "more likely than not" or "with a probability greater than .5."

The word probability can also be used to represent *relative frequency*, in other words, how often an event of interest occurs relative to other possible events. For example, in the case of the first-level supervisors in the agency, our premise told us that 95 out of 100 of these supervisors had taken the basic course in supervision. The relative frequency of 95/100 provided our best estimate of the probability that any one first-level supervisor had attended the training.

We will use the concept of probability throughout this unit on induction and then later in the unit on statistical reasoning.

In the remaining sections we will present some forms within which inductive reasoning can occur. These forms are just a sample of the possible forms. They will be presented first for reasoning about sets and then for reasoning with connectives. Although many of these forms will be very similar to deductive forms, it should be remembered that they differ from deductive forms in terms of the certainty of the conclusion.

Self-Test: Part III.A (answers are given on page 124)

In questions 1 through 7, decide if each of the sentences is true or false.

1. In induction, the premises provide a degree of confirmation for the conclusion.
   (True / false)

2. An inductively correct conclusion is a necessary conclusion; that is, it cannot be false if the premises are true. (True / false)

3. Induction must be based on all available evidence. (True / false)

4. Induction is based on complete evidence. (True / false)

5. A good inductive conclusion should not be altered if new evidence becomes available. (True / false)

6. Probability can be viewed as the degree of confirmation that a set of premises provide for a conclusion. (True / false)

7. Probability may have a numerical value ranging from 0 to 1. (True / false)

8. Given the following premises, decide if each of the conclusions represents an inductive or a deductive conclusion. Then decide if the conclusion represents good reasoning or poor reasoning.

Premises

- Of all individuals who apply to take tests for Federal employment, only about 50% actually report on the scheduled day to take the test.

- Jane and John applied to take a test for a Federal law enforcement job, and they were scheduled to be tested on October 1.

Conclusions

a. It is not true that everyone who applies to take a test for Federal employment reports to take the test on the scheduled date.
(Inductive / deductive) (Good reasoning / poor reasoning)

b. Jane and John will both probably report to take the test on the scheduled date.
(Inductive / deductive) (Good reasoning / poor reasoning)

c. Some people who apply to take a test for Federal employment do not report to take the test on the scheduled date.
(Inductive / deductive) (Good reasoning / poor reasoning)

d. There is a 50% chance that any one applicant will report to take the test on the scheduled date.
(Inductive / deductive) (Good reasoning / poor reasoning)

Part III.B. Inductive Reasoning About Sets

Reasoning about two sets represents a good starting point for talking about induction. Part II.A in the deductive reasoning unit gave you an extensive background that will give you a head start in induction.

Section III.B.1: Inductive Reasoning About Two Sets

Inductive Reasoning About Two Sets When the Universe of Discourse Is Known

In reasoning deductively about the relationships between two sets, we start with one of the basic premises, such as All [members of set A] are [members of set B]. In inductive reasoning we can distinguish two different starting points that pertain to how much we know about one of the sets we are interested in. In other words, we can have different outcomes depending on how much we know about the *universe of discourse* for the set we wish to relate to another set.

The universe of discourse in a deductive or inductive reasoning task is the range of individuals, events, or things about which you wish to draw a conclusion. For an illustration, let us refer to the following premise: "Of all first-line supervisors, 95% have taken the basic supervisory course." The universe of discourse for this statement needs to be defined more explicitly. Clearly, the premise does not refer to all of the first-level supervisors in the world, the nation, or even the Federal Government. In fact, it may apply to first-level supervisors only in one occupation in DHS. Accordingly, let us say that we are referring to the Border Patrol occupation.

If we know how many first-level supervisors exist in the Border Patrol and if we know how many of them belong to the other set we are interested in (people who have taken the basic supervisory course), then we can say that the universe of discourse is *known*. On the other hand, if we do not know how many supervisors there are and if we have obtained information on only some members of the set, then we say that the universe of discourse is *unknown*.

We are in a much stronger position to draw conclusions if the universe of discourse is known than if it is unknown. You will see that we can assign more exact probability values to a prediction if we know the universe of discourse for one of the sets.

Now let us look at the types of conclusions that can be drawn when the universe of discourse is known. First, let us return to the premise about the first-level supervisors. If we can assume that the premise is based on reliable data about all of the first-level supervisors (in other words, the universe of discourse is known), then we can confidently assign a .95 probability to the conclusion that any individual first-line supervisor had taken the basic course. We could represent the reasoning form in the following manner:

Of all first-line supervisors in the Border Patrol, 95% have taken the basic supervisory course.
Pat is a first-line supervisor in the Border Patrol.
Therefore, with a probability of .95, Pat has taken the basic supervisory course.

Now let us see what conclusion we can draw if we are trying to make an inference about an individual who has taken the basic supervisory course. Our premise does not give us complete information about the entire set of people who have taken the course. Therefore, if the only information we have is that a particular person has taken the course, we can conclude that there is some chance that the person is a first-level supervisor in the Border Patrol, but we cannot assign any numerical value or any expression of strength to the probability. We can express this in the following formula:

Of all first-line supervisors in the Border Patrol, 95% have taken the basic supervisory course.
John has taken the basic supervisory course.
Therefore, John may be a first-line supervisor in the Border Patrol,
but the probability is unknown.

Now let us look at another type of scenario in which prediction can be made about an individual's membership in one set based on information about membership in another set. In this scenario, you will have one universal premise (a premise that tells about all the members of a set) and an additional premise that gives a probability that an individual belongs to one of the sets. The following example shows how this scenario would look:

All of the new trainees (in a specific occupation) are college graduates.
There is a 50% chance that your office's new employee this year will be one of the new trainees.
Therefore, the probability that your office will be assigned a college graduate this year is at least 50%.

The probability that your office will be assigned a college graduate might be greater than 50% because there is a chance that your office could be assigned an employee other than a trainee who might also be a college graduate. This unknown probability must be added to the 50% chance of obtaining a trainee (who would definitely be a college graduate). Therefore, the chance of obtaining a college graduate is no lower than .50 and may be higher.

This formula allows you to make an interesting conclusion if the second premise concerns an individual who is in the second set in the original statement, the set of college graduates. Let us assume that the second premise is "There is a 50% chance that your office's new employee will be a college graduate." This information combined with the universal statement "All of our new trainees are college graduates" allows you to conclude that "The probability is no higher than .5 that our new employee will be one of the new trainees." This formula is represented as follows:

All of the new trainees (in a specific occupation) are college graduates.
<u>There is a 50% chance that your office's new employee this year will be a college graduate</u>.
Therefore, the probability is no higher than 50% that your office's new employee will be one of the new trainees.

You are able to reach this conclusion because the universal statement puts an upper limit on the probability that the new employee is a trainee. In other words, this person can only be a new trainee if he or she is a college graduate.

This type of formula -- combining a universal statement about two sets with probabilistic information about an individual -- is a very powerful formula that allows you to draw many conclusions. By working through the exercises in the Self-Test, you will learn about more of these conclusions.

A note about quantities. In discussing probabilities, we have been using various expressions for the size of the probability. The following table shows you some of these expressions and other expressions that are equivalent in meaning.

Degree of probability	Equivalent expressions
Probability greater than .7	greater than a 70% chance
Probability equal to or greater than .7	at least a 70% chance no less than a 70% chance
Probability equal to .7	exactly a 70% chance
Probability equal to or less than .7	up to a 70% chance no greater than a 70% chance no more than a 70% chance
Probability less than .7	less than a 70% chance
Probably	greater than a 50% chance more likely than not

Note: The probability of .7 was used as an example. Any other probability value could be substituted in these expressions.

Inductive Reasoning About Two Sets When the Universe of Discourse Is Unknown

When the universe of discourse is unknown, we must rely on data from specific observations to try to decide what the relationship between the two sets could be. This use of specific observations as the basis for making a general rule is called *inductive generalization*. A simple example about computer diskettes will illustrate the process:

> I have tested every tenth diskette from this shipment and they are all defective.
> Therefore, probably, all diskettes from this shipment are defective.

You can see that the conclusion is inductive. First, it is based on incomplete evidence because I have not tested all of the diskettes from the shipment. Second, the conclusion is only a probable conclusion; it could very well be wrong. If there are any nondefective diskettes in the shipment, then the conclusion is wrong. Obviously this type of reasoning is fraught with danger. No matter how regular events seem to be, there is still a real possibility that such generalizations are wrong.

In spite of the fallibility of inductive generalization, it is a necessary tool for existence in the real world. We must be able to generalize about phenomena rather than treat each event, individual, or thing as if it were different from every other event, individual, or thing.

For example, suppose the law enforcement community refused to make the generalization that every person has distinctive fingerprint patterns simply because the fingerprints of all people (past, present, and future) had not been observed. Clearly, the community would lose a valuable investigative tool. So, the generalization about fingerprints is a highly useful one, even though there may be some (unobserved) exceptions to it.

Statistical reasoning is an aid to inductive generalization when the universe of discourse is unknown. We can think of the universe of discourse as being the same as the statistical idea of a *population*. Random sampling techniques are used to try to obtain a sample of observations that represent the population. The statistics obtained from the sample are evaluated by using statistical models, which estimate the range of likely population values. There are also statistical techniques for making a prediction about an individual, given a generalization about the relationship between two sets.

Statistical reasoning is explained in Unit IV.

Self-Test: Section III.B.1 (answers are on page 124)

1. For the following situations, decide if the universe of discourse is *known* or *unknown*.

    a. A staff officer is writing a report on current and future trends in illegal immigration. In the report the officer must draw some conclusions about the country of origin of all illegal immigrants across the Southwest border. Is the universe of discourse known or unknown for these illegal immigrants?

b. A personnel specialist in Headquarters, who has access to Servicewide personnel records, needs to find out what percentage of the GS-9 employees at DHS are in each of the Officer Corps occupations. Is the universe of discourse known or unknown for GS-9 employees with respect to what occupation they are in?

c. A budget analyst who has agency financial reports must report the proportion of the agency budget that has been spent on travel in the past three fiscal years. Is the universe of discourse known or unknown with respect to total expenditures and the percent spent on travel?

d. A personnel recruitment specialist is interested in knowing how many college seniors read advertisements about DHS jobs that have been placed in collegiate magazines. Her only source of data is information from job applicants about where they learned about DHS job opportunities. Is the universe of discourse known or unknown for the percent of college seniors who read advertisements about DHS jobs?

2. Given the information in the following paragraph, decide which of conclusions *a* through *d* can be correctly inferred.

Paragraph
In the last fiscal year, Sector X added 200 Border Patrol Agents, of which 180 were new hires and 20 were acquired from other sectors. Sector Y acquired 400 new Border Patrol Agents, of which 320 were new hires and 80 were acquired from other sectors.

Conclusions
a. Agent A. B. is one of the new agents in Sector X. Agent A. B. is very likely to be a new hire. (Correct / incorrect)

b. Agent C. D. is one of the new agents in Sector Y. C. D. probably transferred from another sector. (Correct / incorrect)

c. Agent E. F. is a new hire to the Border Patrol. E. F. probably works in Sector Y. (Correct / incorrect)

d. Agent G. H. is a new agent in Sector X. There is only a 10% chance that G. H. transferred from another sector. (Correct / incorrect)

3. Given the information in the following paragraph, decide which of conclusions *a* through *d* can be correctly inferred.

Paragraph

According to records, on a certain vessel entering Long Beach seaport, all of the officers in the crew are from Norway. However, three-fourths of the nonofficer members of the crew are not from Norway. Inspector I. J. is one of the staff assigned to inspect this vessel. Evaluate these conclusions for Inspector I. J.

Conclusions

a. A member of the crew who is a nonofficer has a one-fourth chance of being from Norway. (Correct / incorrect)

b. A randomly selected member of the nonofficer members of the crew has a three-fourths chance of not being from Norway. (Correct / incorrect)

c. A member of the vessel's crew who is from Norway has a three-fourths chance of being an officer. (Correct / incorrect)

d. A member of the vessel's crew who is not from Norway has a three-fourths chance of being an officer. (Correct / incorrect)

4. Given the information in the following paragraph, decide which of conclusions *a* through *d* can be correctly inferred.

Paragraph

At a certain office of an agency, it was standard practice that on their first day in the office all new employees would be given a tour of the office that was the same as the tour given to official visitors. Due to organizational growth, there was a 50% chance on any Monday of the year that a new employee would report for work in the office.

Conclusions

a. On any given Monday, there was at least a 50% chance that someone would be given a tour of the office. (Correct / incorrect)

b. Anyone who was being given a tour of the office on a Monday was most likely a new employee. (Correct / incorrect)

c. The probability that no one would have a tour on any given Monday was no greater than .50. (Correct / incorrect)

d. On any given Monday, there was a 50% chance that there would not be a new employee receiving a tour. (Correct / incorrect)

5. Given the information in the following paragraph, decide which of conclusions *a* through *d* can be correctly inferred.

Paragraph

An administrative officer had to inventory 1,000 items of office equipment prior to a move. He knew that there were exactly 300 pieces of computer equipment, none of which had been declared "surplus." The surplus status of the remaining equipment is unknown prior to inventory. Evaluate these conclusions for the administrative officer.

Conclusions

a. If the administrative officer randomly chose where to begin the inventory, the first piece of equipment to be inventoried would have a 30% or greater chance of not being declared surplus. (Correct / incorrect)

b. The first piece of equipment inventoried had no more than a 70% chance of being declared surplus. (Correct / incorrect)

c. If the first piece of equipment inventoried was one that had been declared surplus, it had a 70% chance of not being computer equipment. (Correct / incorrect)

d. If the first piece of equipment inventoried had not been declared surplus, then the probability that it was computer equipment is completely unknown. (Correct / incorrect)

6. Which of the following statements represent inductive generalizations?

a. All squares have four sides.

b. Moss only grows on the north side of trees.

c. Radiation is harmful to the body.

d. In 1996, there were 50 states in the U. S.A.

Section III.B.2. Advanced Topic -- Inductive Reasoning With More Than Two Sets

Reasoning With More Than Two Sets When the Universe of Discourse Is Known

When the universe of discourse is known, valid forms for reasoning with three sets (these forms, called syllogisms, were introduced in Section II.B.1) can be used as the basis for making predictions about individuals. The following is an example of a form involving three sets:

Ninety percent of our recently hired employees are not certified in CPR.
All of our trainees are recently hired employees.
<u>Sam is one of our trainees.</u>
Therefore, the probability that Sam is not certified in CPR is 90%.

This syllogism has an expression of relative frequency (90%) in the first premise. The second premise is a universal statement about our trainees. The third statement says that Sam is a trainee. From that, we can infer that he is a recently hired employee, and since 90% of recently hired employees are not certified in CPR, we can conclude that there is a 90% chance that Sam is not certified.

Some syllogisms can be used in combination with a probabilistic statement to draw a probabilistic conclusion about an individual. An example is as follows:

No recently hired employee is certified in CPR.
All customer service staff are certified in CPR.
<u>There is a 50% chance that the employee detailed to the emergency site will be a member of the customer service staff.</u>
Therefore, the probability that the person detailed to the emergency site is not a recently hired employee is at least 50%.

If the person detailed to the site has a 50% chance of being from the customer service staff, that person is excluded from the set of recently hired employees with a probability of exactly .5; there is also the possibility that that person is neither a recently hired employee nor a member of the customer service staff. Thus, the probability that the person is not a recently hired employee is no less than .5, and may be greater than .5.

Reasoning About More Than Two Sets When the Universe of Discourse Is Unknown

Logic books describe a type of informal reasoning called *inductive analogy,* which involves reasoning with more than two sets when the universe of discourse is unknown. Stephen Barker, in his text *The Elements of Logic* (1989) represents this type of reasoning as follows:

a, b, c ... each has been observed to be S and P.
<u>k is an S.</u>
Therefore, probably, k is P.

At first this seems to be simply inductive generalization with the added premise "k is an S." But, arguments by analogy depend more on the similarity between a, b, c, and k than they do on the invariance of the relation between S and P. An example of this type of reasoning would be:

Six vans of a certain model, all of which had obstructed windows, were found to be transporting illegal aliens. An agent observes another van of the same model which also has obstructed windows. The agent concludes that the van is probably transporting illegal aliens.

Argument by analogy obviously can be a useful form of reasoning, but like inductive generalization, it can lead to fallacious conclusions.

69

Self-Test: Section III.B.2 (answers are given on page 126)

1. Given the information in the following paragraph, decide which of conclusions *a* through *d* can be correctly inferred.

   Paragraph
   In a work site that was about to be inspected by DHS agents, 30% of the employees were undocumented aliens. None of the undocumented aliens was from a North, South, or Central American country.

   Conclusions
   a. A randomly selected employee from that work site had at least a 30% chance of not being from a North, South, or Central American country. (Correct / incorrect)

   b. Any employee at that site who was from a North, South, or Central American country had a 70% chance of not being an undocumented alien. (Correct / incorrect)

   c. A randomly selected employee from that work site had up to a 70% chance of being from a North, South, or Central American country. (Correct / incorrect)

   d. No one from a North, South, or Central American country worked at this site. (Correct / incorrect)

2. Given the information in the following paragraph, decide which of conclusions *a* through *c* can be correctly inferred.

   Paragraph
   In the newly decorated visitors area, all of the furniture has wood frames rather than plastic. Of all the furniture that was in the visitors area prior to the redecoration, 80% did not have wood frames.

   Conclusions
   a. An item of furniture in the redecorated visitors area has an 80% chance of not being a holdover from before the redecorating. (Correct / incorrect)

   b. An item of furniture that was used in the visitors area before redecoration had no more than a 20% chance of being used in the area after it was redecorated. (Correct / incorrect)

   c. An item of furniture that was used in the visitors area before redecoration has at least an 80% chance of not being used in the area after it was redecorated. (Correct / incorrect)

3. Given the information in the following paragraph, decide which of conclusions *a* through *d* can be correctly inferred.

   Paragraph
   In a one-year time period in a certain district, all cases of suspected document counterfeiting were investigated vigorously. No cases that were investigated vigorously failed to yield a successful prosecution. Agent Z worked in the district during the entire one-year period. That year, a randomly selected case from Agent Z's caseload had a 50% chance of being a case of suspected document counterfeiting.

   Conclusions
   a. This randomly selected case had at least a 50% chance of being investigated vigorously. (Correct / incorrect)

   b. This randomly selected case had at least a 50% chance of not failing to produce a successful prosecution. (Correct / incorrect)

   c. There was exactly a 50% chance that this randomly selected case was not investigated vigorously. (Correct / incorrect)

   d. There was a 50% chance that this case was prosecuted unsuccessfully. (Correct / incorrect)

Part III.C. Inductive Reasoning With Connectives

In exploring inductive reasoning with connectives, we will take the approach, as we did with sets, of exploring the types of inductive conclusions we can reach by adapting the deductive forms.

Section III.C.1: Conditionals With Probabilities

The first form we will study is a conditional in which the consequent is true only with a certain probability when the antecedent is true.[14] Another way of saying this is that the consequent is true for only a proportion of the time when the antecedent is true. This means that part of the time the antecedent will be true and the consequent will be untrue. (This concept will be studied again as the topic of *conditional probability* in the unit on statistical reasoning.)

---

[14] **Logic Note.** Remember that the antecedent of the conditional is the "if" part of the sentence and the consequent is the "then" part of the sentence.

The following example illustrates this type of conditional:

> If an agent applies for every vacancy in Sector X, he or she will have a 30% chance of being promoted in Sector X this year.
> Agent Jones will apply for every vacancy in Sector X this year.
> _____
> Therefore, Agent Jones will have a 30% chance of being promoted in Sector X this year.

Notice how different this formula is from the conditional used in deduction. The formula yields only a probabilistic conclusion. Agent Jones may or may not be promoted in Sector X if she applies for every vacancy.

Unlike the deductive conditional, this form does not permit a definite conclusion to be drawn if the consequent is denied.[15] In other words, from the information that an agent was *not* promoted, we cannot draw a conclusion about the probability that the agent applied for every vacancy.

Like the deductive conditional, this form does not permit a conclusion if the antecedent is negated (the inverse) or the consequent is affirmed (the converse). In other words, from information that an agent did not apply for all vacancies in Sector X, we would not be able to estimate the likelihood that the agent was not promoted in Sector X (the inverse). From information that the agent was promoted in Sector X, we would not be able to estimate the probability that the agent applied for all vacancies in Sector X (the converse).

It is interesting to note here that the probability that an event will not occur is equal to 1 minus the probability that it will occur. Therefore, we can conclude that if a person does apply for every vacancy, the person has a 70% chance of **not** being promoted. We can say that these two probabilities (.3 and .7) are the *complements* of each other, because the two probabilities add up to 1.

The Biconditional With Probabilities

We can define a biconditional premise that has two conditional probabilities associated with it. It would retain the symmetry associated with the deductive biconditional. Such a biconditional would look like this:

---

[15] **Logic Note**. Another way of saying this is that the *contrapositive* is not a valid conclusion from this type of conditional.

If a person has a certain type of infection, diagnostic test A has a 90% chance of giving a positive diagnosis.

If a person (whose infection status is unknown) receives a positive diagnosis on test A, there is a 90% chance that the person has this type of infection.[16]

Individual B is known to have this type of infection.
Therefore, individual B has a 90% chance of receiving a positive diagnosis on test A.

The valid conclusion shown above is based on affirming the first part of this biconditional. Another valid conclusion would be:

Individual C (whose infection status is unknown) has received a positive diagnosis on test A.
Therefore, individual C has a 90% chance of having this type of infection.

Like the inductive conditional, this form still would not give a definite conclusion if either the antecedent or the consequent were negated. In other words, from the information that a person did not have this type of infection, we would not be able to draw any conclusion about the probability that the person would have a positive diagnosis on test A. From information that a person received a negative diagnosis on test A, we would not be able to draw a conclusion about the probability that the person had the infection. Therefore, this biconditional has some limitations on the types of conclusions that can be drawn, in contrast to the deductive biconditional.

Self-Test: Section III.C.1 (answers are given on page 127)

1. The following paragraph contains a conditional statement with a probability. Given the information in the paragraph, decide which of conclusions *a* through *d* are correct inferences.

   Paragraph
   In a certain sector it was found that if a vehicle transporting illegal aliens was apprehended within the sector by any law enforcement authority, there was a 20% chance that it was stopped for speeding. Vehicle A was apprehended by a law enforcement officer and was found to be transporting illegal aliens. Vehicle B was also transporting illegal aliens, but it was not apprehended.

---

[16] **Logic Note.** For purposes of simplicity, the same probability (.90) is used for the two parts of the biconditional. However, different probabilities could be used for the two parts.

Conclusions
a. There is a 20% chance that vehicle A was stopped for speeding.
   (Correct / incorrect)

b. There is an 80% chance that vehicle B was not stopped for speeding.
   (Correct / incorrect)

c. There is an 80% chance that vehicle A was not stopped for speeding.
   (Correct / incorrect)

d. Of all vehicles stopped for speeding in this sector, 20% were transporting illegal
   aliens. (Correct / incorrect)

2. The following paragraph contains a biconditional with a probability. Given the
   information in the paragraph, decide which of conclusions *a* through *d* are correct
   inferences.

Paragraph
A librarian in a law enforcement agency, after studying circulation records and
surveying users, was able to draw two conclusions about library use. First, if a book was
checked out of the library for use on a specific work project, there was a 70% chance
that it would be returned on time. Also, of all the books that were returned on time, 70%
had been signed out for use on a specific work project.

Conclusions
a. If a book was signed out for some reason other than a specific work project, there
   was a 70% chance that it would not be returned on time. (Correct / incorrect)

b. Of 1,000 books returned on time in a one-month period, probably about 700 of them
   were signed out for use on a specific work project. (Correct / incorrect)

c. In one month, 500 books were signed out for specific work projects, and thus it can
   be expected that approximately 350 of them will be returned on time.
   (Correct / incorrect)

d. If a book was not returned on time, it was more likely than not signed out for a
   reason other than a specific work project. (Correct / incorrect)

Section III.C.2: Connectives With an Added Premise Containing a Probability

Now let us look at another way of using the conditional in induction. As we did for sets, we
can combine information from a deductive conditional (if p then q) with probabilistic

information about the occurrence of the antecedent, p. Then we can draw an inductive conclusion about the probability of the occurrence of the consequent, q.

In the example below, we use the conditional from the deductive reasoning section and add a probabilistic premise:

> If there is a credible bomb threat to a Federal office building, then the building is always evacuated until a search is completed.
>
> A Federal office building has a 1% chance of receiving a credible bomb threat sometime within a year.
> Therefore, a Federal office building has at least a 1% chance of being evacuated during a year's time.

The conclusion has the probability value of **at least** 1% because the building may have some likelihood of being evacuated for reasons other than a bomb threat. That probability is not contained in the information that our premises give us, but we must allow for it in our conclusion.

Now let us vary this formula by combining the conditional with information about the probability that the consequent is true. Suppose we have information that "the chance that a Federal office building will be evacuated for a search at some point during the year is 1%." We can then conclude that the chance that a credible bomb threat is made to a Federal building is no greater than 1%. This formula can be expressed as follows:

> If there is a credible bomb threat to a Federal office building, then the building is always evacuated until a search is completed.
>
> The chance that a Federal office building will be evacuated for a search at some point during the year is 1%.
> Therefore, the chance that a credible bomb threat will be made to a Federal building is no greater than 1% in a year.

This conclusion is true because the 1% chance of evacuation includes evacuations due to credible bomb threats and any other causes. The conditional statement tells us that there will not be a credible bomb threat without an evacuation of the building. So, the upper limit on the chance of a bomb threat is 1%.

When a conditional is combined with an added probabilistic premise about either the antecedent or the consequent, there is always a conclusion that has a range of probabilities.

We will illustrate the remaining conclusions through the use of formulas based on the example above. (Further real-life examples of these formulas will be found in the Self-

75

Test.) The first is the formula that applies when you know the probability that the antecedent is not true:

> If there is a credible bomb threat to a Federal office building, then the building is always evacuated until a search is completed.
>
> <u>A Federal office building has a 99% chance of **not** receiving a credible bomb threat sometime within a year.</u>
> Therefore, a Federal office building has no more than a 99% chance of **not** being evacuated during a year's time.

Since the building has a 99% chance of not receiving a credible bomb threat, it has a 1% chance of receiving such a threat and thus being evacuated. This relationship puts an upper limit of 99% on the probability that the building will not be evacuated. In addition, there is some (unknown) chance of its being evacuated for some other reason. Therefore, the probability that the building will not be evacuated might be lower than 99%.

The next formula applies when you know the probability that the consequent is not true:

> If there is a credible bomb threat to a Federal office building, then the building is always evacuated until a search is completed.
>
> <u>The chance that a Federal office building will not be evacuated for a search at some point during the year is 99%.</u>
> Therefore, the chance that a credible bomb threat will not be made to a Federal building is equal to or greater than 99% in a year.

If the second premise is true, there is a 1% chance that the building will be evacuated for a search at some point during the year. This means that there is no more than a 1% chance that a credible bomb threat will be made and thus no less than a 99% chance that such a bomb threat will *not* be made.

Biconditionals

When a biconditional is used with an added premise containing a probability, the resulting conclusion has a specific probability rather than a range of probability. Let us illustrate this with the following biconditional statement:

> The Secretary of DHS is the director of your agency if and only if you are an employee of DHS.
>
> <u>There is a 60% chance that a person attending this conference is an employee of DHS.</u>
> Therefore, there is a 60% chance that the Secretary of DHS is the agency director of a person attending this conference.

76

This formula is reversible; in other words, you can begin with information about the probability that the Secretary of DHS is the agency director of a person attending this conference and conclude that the person has the same probability of being an employee of DHS.

You can also draw conclusions if you have information that the antecedent or the consequent is not true. For example, suppose you have the information that "There is a 30% chance that a student in this computer training course is not an employee of DHS." From that information, you could conclude that "There is a 30% chance that the Secretary of DHS is not the agency director of a student in this computer training course." This type of formula will be used in exercise 3 in the Self-Test.

Advanced Topic: Other Connectives

Extended connectives based on the conditional can be used with added probabilistic premises. So can compound connectives that are based on the conditional (see exercise 4 in the Self-Test). However, the other connectives, such as alternations and conjunctions, cannot be adapted so easily because they entail computations with the probabilities. This topic will be discussed in the unit on statistical reasoning.

Self-Test: Section III.C.2 (answers are given on page 128)

1. The following paragraph contains a conditional premise and an added premise with a probability. Given the information in the paragraph, decide which of conclusions *a* through *c* are correct.

   Paragraph
   In one district, the Detention and Deportation staff had a busy caseload of criminal and noncriminal alien cases in which deportation procedures were pending. If an alien in one of these cases was a criminal, he or she was not detained at the DHS detention facility. Instead, criminal aliens were placed in county jails. In this district, one-tenth of all cases concerned criminal aliens.

   Conclusions
   a. A case in this district had at least a 10% chance of not involving someone who was detained at the DHS detention facility. (Correct / incorrect)

   b. A case in this district had no more than a 90% chance of involving someone who was detained at the DHS detention facility. (Correct / incorrect)

   c. A case in this district had less than a 90% chance of concerning a noncriminal alien. (Correct / incorrect)

2. The following paragraph contains a conditional premise and an added premise with a probability. Given the information in the paragraph, decide which of conclusions *a* through *c* are correct.

Paragraph

If an employee contributes to the Combined Federal Campaign through payroll deduction, there is a record of a special deduction on the employee's biweekly earnings statement. In a certain agency, there was a 90% chance that any randomly selected employee had a record of some kind of special deduction on his or her earnings statement.

Conclusions

a. There is at least a 10% chance that a randomly selected employee does not contribute to the Combined Federal Campaign through payroll deduction. (Correct / incorrect)

b. There is a 10% or greater chance that a randomly selected employee did contribute to the Combined Federal Campaign through payroll deduction. (Correct / incorrect)

c. There is a 10% chance that a randomly selected employee did not have a special deduction on his or her biweekly earnings statement. (Correct / incorrect)

3. The following paragraph contains a biconditional premise and an added premise with a probability. Given the information in the paragraph, decide which of conclusions *a* through *c* are correct.

Paragraph

Employees in a certain category are eligible for overtime pay if and only if they work more than eight hours in one day. Records showed that one employee in this category worked more than eight hours on one-fourth of her regular work days in the last year.

Conclusions

a. There was more than a 25% chance that this employee was eligible for overtime pay on any randomly selected day. (Correct / incorrect)

b. There was a 75% chance that this employee was not eligible for overtime pay on any randomly selected day. (Correct / incorrect)

c. The chance that this employee was eligible for overtime pay on any randomly selected day was 25%. (Correct / incorrect)

4. **Advanced Exercise:** The following paragraph contains a compound conditional premise and an added premise with a probability. Given the information in the paragraph, decide which of conclusions *a* through *c* are correct.

Paragraph
In a study of 500 work stations that had problems with LAN access, it was decided that if the work stations got certain new hardware or upgraded software, the problems would be corrected. After six months had elapsed, it was found that for 40% of the work stations, the problems had not been corrected.

Conclusions
a. For any given work station, there was a 20% chance that it had not gotten new hardware and a 20% chance that it had not gotten upgraded software.
   (Correct / incorrect)

b. For any given work station, the probability was 60% that it had gotten both the new hardware and the upgraded software. (Correct / incorrect)

c. For any given work station, the probability was at least .4 that it had gotten neither the specified new hardware nor the upgraded software. (Correct / incorrect)

Part III.D. Fallacies in Induction

Just as there are prevalent fallacies in deduction, which we called illogical biases, so there are fallacies in induction. First, there are what might be called "schematic" fallacies, involving incorrect conclusions about converses, inverses, and other forms. The inductive biases are related to the corresponding deductive biases, but they are not always the same.

Next, there are biases in interpreting probabilistic data from real-life observations. These will be covered in the unit on statistical reasoning. These biases arise because, in trying to interpret the mass of information that we take in everyday, we make various types of errors. All of these errors violate one or more of the rules for statistical reasoning.

Finally, there are errors of inductive reasoning that the logician Stephen Barker (1989) calls *pure fallacies of induction*. We will take a little time to review these because they provide important cautions. There are three of these fallacies, as follows:

- forgetful induction: neglecting to use some of the information that you possess
- hasty induction: basing a conclusion on very slight evidence
- slothful induction: treating a conclusion as though it were less probable than it really is

79

The following is an example of forgetful induction, because the reasoner neglects some important information and draws a conclusion using only a small part of the available information:

> "Ninety-five percent of the new vehicles we purchased last year performed very well. Almost all of our officers expressed satisfaction with them. However, recently I received a report that one officer drove three different new vehicles that had mechanical problems. Therefore, I doubt that these vehicles are reliable enough for our use."

The reasoner is neglecting the information about 95% of the new vehicles we purchased last year and is only attending to the report about three vehicles.

The next paragraph shows an example of hasty induction, because the reasoner bases a conclusion on slender evidence:

> "The only time that I attended training on computer applications the instructor was poor and I didn't learn anything. Therefore, computer training seems valueless, and I don't plan to attend it again."

Slothful induction is represented by the following reasoning:

> "The opinion polls by all the major polling organizations show that the incumbent will win re-election to this office. However, I still don't think it is very likely that the incumbent will win."

Slothful induction tends to occur when the reasoner is reluctant to believe the conclusion, regardless of the evidence.

All of these fallacies violate the requirement to use all the available evidence in forming an inductive conclusion. Both hasty induction and slothful induction also violate the cardinal rule that the degree of the probability claimed for the conclusion must be supported by the premises.

Reference for Unit III

Barker, Stephen F. (1989). *The Elements of Logic*, 5th edition. New York: McGraw-Hill.

Unit IV - Induction 2: Statistical Reasoning and Estimating Probability

In your job, you need to follow the basic rules of statistical reasoning and probability every day. In fact, it is the correct application of these rules that improves the accuracy with which you can make generalizations based on information you receive while performing your job. The purpose of this unit is to familiarize you with the basic principles of statistical and probability theory. In the last part of the unit, heuristics or rules of thumb that often lead to erroneous generalizations are discussed so that you can avoid these statistical illogical biases while performing your job.

Part IV.A. Populations and Samples

Every day, you make inferences about the probability that an *event* will occur. The term event covers just about anything you can think of. For example, an illegal entry into the United States, a promotion, and the purchase of new computer equipment are all events. The entire collection of the events of interest is referred to as the *population*[17]. In some cases, the population is small and easily observed, such as the number of absences among agents in a particular Border Patrol station. Other times, the population is large, making it difficult to observe all events, such as the number of absences among all employees working in the United States.

When the population is large, it is impractical to attempt to observe all possible events. Instead, inferences about the probability that an event will occur are made on the basis of a *sample* of observed events from the population. The term sample refers to a subset of all events in the population. For example, news programs often conduct exit polls to project the winner of an election before all the votes are counted. Since a large number of people vote in an election, polls are conducted using a sample of all voters.

The extent to which a sample reflects the population has major implications for the accuracy of the inferences you draw from the sample. For example, in 1948 the Chicago Tribune conducted a poll to project the winner of the presidential election. Since the results of the poll showed that Thomas Dewey had defeated incumbent Harry Truman, the Chicago Tribune decided to use "Dewey Defeats Truman" as the headline for the morning edition of the newspaper. Unfortunately for the Chicago Tribune, the sample of voters included in their poll did not accurately reflect the population of all voters. The final results of the election showed that Harry Truman had won 303 electoral votes to Thomas Dewey's 189 (Strom Thurmond won 39 electoral votes running on the States' Rights Democratic ticket). As a result, the Chicago Tribune suffered an embarrassing blow when Harry Truman held a copy of the newspaper over his head after the election. This part of the unit presents basic

---

[17] Although we are used to thinking of the term population as referring to people, in statistics the term can refer to any events of interest.

rules of statistical reasoning which maximize the likelihood that a sample reflects the population (and minimize the likelihood of making a mistake similar to that made by the Chicago Tribune in 1948).

Section IV.A.1. Law of Large Numbers

The *law of large numbers* states that a sample is more likely to reflect the population when the sample contains a large rather than small number of observations. For example, imagine you are a supervisor and are asked to evaluate the quality of 50 graduates of a training class, two of whom are assigned to your district. You are very impressed with the performance of the two graduates, but you decide to obtain additional information before making an evaluation. You call a supervisor at Alpha District who has been assigned ten graduates of the training class. The supervisor tells you that he finds the graduates to be average performers. Which sample is more likely to reflect the population of 50 graduates of the training class?

While you are impressed with the quality of the two graduates assigned to your district, it would be premature to make an evaluation of the entire training class on the basis of their performance. According to the law of large numbers, the likelihood that a sample reflects the population increases with the size of the sample. Therefore, the evaluation made by the supervisor at Alpha District (based on the performance of ten graduates) is more likely to reflect the quality of graduates of the training class than your evaluation (based on the performance of two graduates).

The law of large numbers also states that estimates based on small samples are more likely to be influenced by extreme observations (that is, observations that differ greatly from the typical occurrence in the population) than are estimates based on large samples. For example, imagine that your favorite baseball player had a batting average of .300 (an average of 3 hits in every 10 official times at bat) during the past season. If you look at the player's batting average during individual games, you would find a number of games in which his average was .000 (for example, no hits in four official times at bat), as well as a number of games in which his average was 1.000 (for example, four hits in four official times at bat). On the other hand, if you looked at the player's batting average over the course of ten games, it is unlikely that his average was .000 (for example, no hits in 40 official times at bat), or 1.000 (for example, 40 hits in 40 official times at bat). Therefore, you are more likely to find extreme batting averages during individual games than you are over the course of ten games.

While there are statistics that estimate the likelihood that a sample represents the population, a presentation of these statistics is beyond the scope of this unit. However, it is important that you understand the relationship between the size of the population and the sample size necessary to maximize the likelihood that the sample reflects the population. For extremely large populations, such as the population of all eligible voters in the United States, a sample of less than 1% of the population may be sufficient. In fact, polls conducted to predict who will win a presidential election are often based on a sample of 10,000 out of a population of 100,000,000 eligible voters. When the population is relatively small, such as the population of 50 graduates of a training class described above, a sample of at least 30% of the population may be necessary. Therefore, as the size of the population decreases, there is an increase in the percentage of observed events in the population required to ensure that the sample represents the population.

Self-Test: Section IV.A.1 (answers are given on page 130)

The problems below require you to apply the law of large numbers. Try to determine the correct answer before reading the explanation given at the end of the manual.

1. In order to get information about a car he is interested in purchasing, John buys a copy of *Car and Driver* magazine containing a survey on owner satisfaction. For each car, 1,000 owners participated in the survey. The results of the survey suggest that 80% of the people who own the type of car John is interested in purchasing are satisfied.

   While at work the next day, John is talking with three of his coworkers and tells them he intends to purchase the car. It turns out that two of the coworkers have friends who own the car and both coworkers claim that their friends are dissatisfied with its performance. Should John consider buying the car? Justify your answer by applying the law of large numbers.

   _____

   _____

   _____

   _____

   _____

2. The ACME Corporation has two claims processing centers. Center A processes 1,000 claims a day, while Center B processes 100 claims a day. At each center, it is estimated that an average of 5% of the claims processed each day are incorrect. Beginning next year, ACME's Quality Control Division will be tracking the percentage of incorrect claims processed daily at each center in order to get a more accurate estimate. Which center is more likely to have days on which 7.5% or more of the claims processed are incorrect? Justify your answer by applying the law of large numbers.

   _____

   _____

   _____

   _____

   _____

Section IV.A.2. Sample Representativeness

Another factor that impacts whether a sample reflects the population of events is *sample representativeness*. According to the rule of sample representativeness, samples that are similar to the population in terms of characteristics relevant to the event you are measuring are more likely to be representative of the population. One way to ensure sample representativeness is through *random sampling*. A sample is random if all possible events in the population have an equal chance of being observed.

A type of random sampling, called *stratified random sampling*, involves sampling randomly from sub-populations identified on the basis of key characteristics of the population. For example, imagine you are interested in identifying the concerns of all employees in your sector. Your sector has three stations, with 60% of the employees in Station 1, 20% of the employees in Station 2, and 20% of the employees in Station 3. In the past, you have noticed that employees in each station tend to have different concerns. One way to ensure that each station is represented in the sample is to select employees randomly from each station so that 60% of the sample is from Station 1, 20% of the sample is from Station 2, and 20% of the sample is from Station 3.

People who are not familiar with the importance of sample representativeness often base their inferences on *biased* samples. A sample is biased when it does not reflect the population on relevant characteristics. For example, because the media report routinely on political scandals, some people assume that all politicians are crooked, even though very few politicians are ever involved in a scandal.

The impact of sampling bias can also be demonstrated using the example of the 50 graduates of a training class presented earlier. Imagine that the top 25 ranked graduates of the training class are assigned to your district. After one month on the job, you find that most of the 25 graduates are superior performers. While it may be tempting to give the entire training class an excellent evaluation, remember that the graduates assigned to your district represent the top performers in the training class. Your evaluation might not be as favorable if the 25 graduates assigned to your district were ranked at the bottom of the training class.

In some cases, sampling bias can negate the benefits gained by satisfying the law of large numbers and vice versa. In the training class example above, an evaluation made on the basis of the 25 top ranked graduates of the training class satisfies the law of large numbers, while violating the rule of sample representativeness. On the other hand, an evaluation made on the basis of the performance of three graduates of the training class assigned randomly to your district would satisfy the rule of sample representativeness, while violating the law of large numbers. The best estimate of the quality of the graduates of the training class would be obtained by observing a large number of high, medium, and low ranked graduates selected randomly from the training class.

Self-Test: Section IV.A.2 (answers are given on page 130)

The problems below require you to apply the rule of sample representativeness. Try to determine the correct answer before reading the explanation given at the end of the manual.

1. While reading the newspaper, Randy comes across an article that describes the results of a poll asking people whom they intend to vote for in an upcoming local election. According to the article, the sample was drawn by selecting telephone numbers randomly from the telephone book. The results of the survey suggest that the incumbent is in a close race with the challenger, with both candidates getting approximately 50% of the votes.

   The next day, Randy is watching a local television news program that conducted a similar poll on the upcoming election. Viewers participated in the poll by calling a 1-900 number at a cost of $.50. The results of the poll suggest that the incumbent would get 60% of the votes, a comfortable margin of victory. Which poll should Randy consider to be more accurate? Justify your answer by applying the rule of sample representativeness.

   _____

   _____

   _____

   _____

   _____

2. Lisa is a manager in a district with 500 employees. Due to an unusually high amount of turnover, the district is almost always understaffed. While in the past managers could fill open shifts by requiring employees to work overtime, the recent union contract makes overtime voluntary.

   In order to gauge available staff hours, the District Director asks Lisa to estimate the percentage of employees in the district who would be willing to work overtime. Lisa asks 10 employees working in her office if they would be willing to work overtime. Much to her satisfaction, 8 of the employees say they would be willing to work overtime.

   Later that day, a coworker tells Lisa he feels it will be difficult to get enough volunteers to fill the open shifts. He states that only 3 of the 10 employees he spoke with are willing to work overtime. Lisa's coworker surveyed employees working during different shifts in key areas within the district. Which estimate should Lisa present to the District Director? Justify your answer by applying the rule of sample representativeness.

_____

_____

_____

_____

_____

_____

Section IV.A.3. Regression to the Mean

The term *regression to the mean* can be defined two ways. First, regression to the mean can refer to the fact that, on average, an extreme observation of an event will be followed by a less extreme observation of the same event. That is, subsequent observations of the event are likely to be more similar to the typical occurrence in the population. Regression to the mean occurs when chance factors have an extremely negative (or extremely positive) impact on the initial observation. For example, imagine you are the police commissioner in a major U.S. city and would like to test the effectiveness of a new technique you have developed to reduce crime. You decide to try the technique in the five precincts with the highest crime rate during the past month. A month after introducing the new technique, you find that the crime rate has gone down in four of the five precincts where the new technique has been implemented.

Making an assessment at this point would be unwise because a number of chance factors could have accounted for the reduced crime rate in the four precincts (for example, poor weather keeping people off the streets for most of the month). The best way to evaluate the effectiveness of the crime reduction technique would be to implement it in a large number of randomly selected precincts. This satisfies both the law of large numbers and the rule of sample representativeness and helps prevent you from making an erroneous evaluation based on the regression to the mean phenomenon. If, over time, the crime rate goes down in all precincts, you can conclude that the technique is effective. However, if the only precincts to show improvement are those with a high crime rate during the month prior to implementing the technique, the reduction in crime can be attributed to the phenomenon of regression to the mean.

The second definition of regression to the mean refers to the fact that, on average, an extreme observation of one event will be associated with a less extreme observation of a different, but related event. For example, imagine you are assigned the 10 highest ranked graduates of a training class. You are told that graduates with a high class rank during training tend to be better performers on the job than graduates with a low class rank. On the basis of this information, you estimate that the graduates will be among the best performers in your district. While this estimate would be justified, it is important to keep in mind that the relationship between training class rank and on-the-job performance is not perfect. As a result, there will be instances where graduates with a low class rank turn out to be good performers, as well as instances where graduates with a high class rank turn out to be poor performers.

86

This phenomenon often occurs in colleges where class rank in high school is used to select applicants for admission each year. Since high school rank and college performance are not *perfectly* related, there will always be exceptions to the rule that applicants with a high class rank will be good students, and applicants with a low class rank will be poor students.

Self-Test: Section IV.A.3 (answers are given on page 131)

The problems below require you to identify the regression to the mean phenomenon. Try to determine the correct answer before reading the explanation given at the end of the manual.

1. Laura has developed a course outline that details an approach to teaching that she claims will increase students' scores on a standardized test. Eager to see if the teaching approach is successful, Laura's supervisor assigns her to teach the course to 20 students who scored in the bottom 10% of all test takers on a recent administration of the standardized test. After completing the course, the students' test scores increased an average of 20 points, with most students now scoring in the bottom 30% of all test takers. Despite the positive results, Laura warns her supervisor that it is premature to call the course a success. Do you agree with Laura that it is premature to claim that the course is effective in increasing scores on the standardized test? Justify your answer considering the regression to the mean phenomenon.

_____

_____

_____

_____

_____

2. Greg is interested in seeing a movie with his friend Jane. While looking through the newspaper, Greg comes across a new movie he would really like to see. Unfortunately, Jane is skeptical about going to see the movie because it stars a stand-up comedian. Eager to see the movie, Greg points out that many stand-up comedians have gone on to become Jane's favorite actors. Convinced that a good stand-up comedian will be a good actor, Jane agrees to go to the movie with Greg.

After the movie, both Greg and Jane comment on how disappointed they were with the acting ability of the stand-up comedian. Should Greg and Jane be surprised that the stand-up comedian's acting ability was not as good as his ability to deliver a funny comedy routine? Justify your answer considering the regression to the mean phenomenon.

_____

_____

_____

_____

_____

Section IV.A.4. Sample Validity

Sample validity refers to the extent to which a sample of observed events reflects what interests you about the population. For example, imagine you are asked to determine the best way to evaluate the performance of graduates of a training class. A large number of graduates of the training class (law of large numbers) have been assigned randomly to work in your district (sample representativeness). Aware of the rules of statistical reasoning, you feel comfortable that the sample reflects the population of graduates of the training class. You then set out to determine the best way to evaluate performance. You decide to use specific aspects of the job performed by experienced employees as your measure of performance.

While it is likely that the sample reflects the population of graduates of the training class, your definition of performance is questionable. By focusing on activities performed by experienced employees, you may make an invalid evaluation of the performance of the graduates. A more valid way to measure the performance of graduates of the training class would be to use job activities that are not impacted by experience.

Self-Test: Section IV.A.4 (answers are given on page 131)

Below are two problems that require you to apply the rule of sample validity. Try to determine the correct answer before reading the explanation given at the end of the manual.

1. Julia is interested in buying a new stereo system. She listens to a number of stereo systems and has a difficult time determining which is best. Julia decides that the most accurate way to assess the quality of a stereo system is cost. She reasons that the most expensive stereo system must be the best, or it would not cost more money than the other stereo systems. Do you agree with Julia's belief that the best stereo system is the one that costs the most money? Justify your answer by applying the rule of sample validity.

_____

_____

_____

_____

_____

88

2. David is asked to assess whether employees in his district are satisfied with their pay. In order to make this assessment, David uses the results of a recently conducted survey on overall job satisfaction of employees in his district. The survey sample was large and representative of all employees in his district. The results of the survey showed that 85% of the employees in David's district are satisfied overall with their job. David concludes that if employees are satisfied with their job overall, they must be satisfied with their pay. He tells his supervisor that most employees are satisfied with their pay. Do you agree with David's conclusion that employees who are satisfied overall with their job are satisfied with their pay? Justify your answer by applying the rule of sample validity.

_____

_____

_____

_____

_____

Section IV.A.5. Summary

In this part of the unit, a number of rules of statistical reasoning were presented. Since you are often faced with situations that require you to consider a sample of all possible events, understanding these rules can increase the likelihood that your sample reflects the population of interest. Below is a list of tips that can help you when applying these rules while performing your job.

- Clearly define the population of interest. It is in your best interest to define the population as narrowly as possible. This helps to ensure that you are obtaining relevant information, and makes drawing a sample more manageable.

- Determine the number of observations you need to make in order to get an accurate reflection of the population. Remember, when a population is small, you may have to observe a larger portion of the population in order to draw an accurate conclusion.

- Define the key characteristics of the population you are interested in. Determine if your sample of observations reflects the population in terms of these characteristics.

- Ensure that what you are observing reflects what you are interested in.

Part IV.B. Estimating Probability

We live in a *probabilistic* world in which very few things happen with complete certainty. For example, most people expect to be able to take a particular route to work each day. However, sometimes people are forced to take an alternate route due to accidents or road construction. Thus, we expect to able to take our usual route to work, but we know that there may be occasions when we will have to take an alternate route. Understanding basic rules of probability will help you make better estimates about the likelihood that events will occur. This part of the unit outlines some of the basic concepts and rules of probability and shows how they are related to making inferences in your job.

Section IV.B.1. Probability Defined

As mentioned in Unit III, a probability ranges from 0 to 1, with "0" representing an event that will definitely not occur, ".5" representing an event that is as likely to occur as it is not to occur, and "1" representing an event that will definitely occur. In everyday life, the term "chance" is often used as an expression of probability. For example, when a weather reporter talks about the likelihood of rain, he or she typically states "there is a 50% chance of rain" rather than "the probability that it will rain is .5". Therefore, probability will be expressed as chance in this unit to keep consistent with the expression of probability in everyday life.

Section IV.B.2. Base Rate Information and Probability Estimates

An estimate about the probability that an event will occur is often based on information from a variety of sources. An important piece of information, which is often overlooked, is the *base rate.* The base rate is also called the *prior probability* because it refers to the number of times an event has occurred in the past. For example, imagine you play tennis with a friend once a week. On average, you win two of the four games played. Therefore, the base rate of games you win while playing tennis with your friend is 50%.

The base rate is especially useful in two situations. First, the base rate is used when additional information is not available. For example, imagine you are in charge of security for a facility near a seaside resort. The manager of the facility asks you to estimate how many crimes will be committed during the summer season. If no other information is available, your estimate should be based on the crime rate during previous summer seasons (note that the term crime rate is used instead of base rate).

The base rate is also used when additional information provided is unreliable. Using the example above, imagine you are provided with a schedule for the summer season. You notice that an unusually large number of conventions are scheduled throughout the summer. In the past, crime rates have tended to increase during conventions. However, the increase in crime during conventions has varied from year to year. Information about previous crime rates when conventions are held can be used to adjust your base rate estimate of the crime rate during the summer season.

Section IV.B.3. Occurrence of Two or More Events

When considering the probability that two events will occur, it is important to identify their relationship to each other. Two events are considered *independent* when the occurrence of one event is unrelated to the occurrence of another event. For example, the probability of having red hair is independent of gender, with men being just as likely to have red hair as women. Two events are considered *dependent* when the occurrence of one event is related to the occurrence of another event. For example, the probability of being over six feet tall is dependent on gender, with men being more likely than women to be over six feet tall.

The occurrence of two events can be expressed as either a *joint probability* or a *conditional probability*. Joint probability refers to the probability that two events will occur at the same time. For example, the probability of being male *and* being over six feet tall is a joint probability. Typically, joint probability is denoted as p(A,B). Thus, p(over six feet tall, male) is used to represent the joint probability of being a male and being over six feet tall.

Conditional probability refers to the probability that one event will occur given that some other event has occurred. For example, the probability of being over six feet tall *given* being a male is a conditional probability. Typically, conditional probability is denoted as p(A/B), where "/" represents the word "given." Thus, p(over six feet tall/male) is used to represent the conditional probability of being over six feet tall given being a male. Conditional probability is especially useful when two events are not independent, such as the relationship between height and gender.[18]

Section IV.B.4. Multiplicative Rules of Probability

The *multiplicative rule for independent events* states that the probability that two independent events will occur is equal to the product of their individual probabilities. For example, imagine you are the chief of police in a major U.S. city. Determined to live up to her campaign promise, the mayor of the city asks you to develop a comprehensive plan that will reduce crime. After drafting a plan, you realize that the success of the plan depends on both an increase in the number of police officers in the city and an improvement in the economy. While you have little control over these factors, you do know that there is a 70% chance that new officers will be hired, and a 30% chance that the economy will improve.

---

[18] **Logic Note.** Notice that conditional probability expresses the relationship of a probabilistic conditional statement discussed in Unit III. Also, while the symbol "p" is typically used to represent probability, you can also use the abbreviation "prob" if you are using symbols to represent connectives such as the conditional. For example, you could represent a conditional with probability as: If p, then q (prob=.50).

You also know that the state of the economy will have no impact on whether or not new officers are hired. In probability, these events are represented as:

p(new officers) = 70%
p(improvement in the economy) = 30%

The joint probability that both new police officers are hired and the economy is improved is determined by applying the multiplicative rule for independent events as follows:

p(new officers, improvement in the economy) = p(new police officers) X p(improvement in the economy)

Thus, according to the multiplicative rule for independent events, there is a 21% chance (70% X 30%) that both new police officers are hired and the economy is improved.[19]

When two events are not independent, the ***multiplicative rule for dependent events*** is used to account for the fact that the two events are related. According to the multiplicative rule for dependent events, the probability of two dependent events occurring is equal to the product of the individual probability that one event will occur and the conditional probability that the second event will occur given that the first event has occurred. For example, imagine you and your neighbor work in different departments for the same agency. In order to save money, you and your neighbor carpool to work. Recently, your agency announced that it is opening a new office complex closer to your home and intends to transfer two of its six departments to the new office complex. You are interested in transferring to the new complex, but would like to continue carpooling with your neighbor.

The probability that both you and your neighbor are transferred to the new office complex is dependent because once one department is transferred, the probability that the second department is transferred is reduced. The reduction in the probability that the second department is transferred occurs because there is one less opening at the new office complex and one less unit to fill it (1 opening / 5 departments). As a result, there is a 20% chance that the second department is transferred to the new office complex given that one department has already been transferred. In probability, these events are represented as:

p(a department is transferred) = 33%
p(a department is transferred / a department has already been transferred) = 20%

In this case, the probability that both you and your neighbor are transferred to the new office complex is determined by applying the multiplicative rule of probability for dependent events as follows:

p(your department is transferred, your neighbor's department is transferred) =
p(a department is transferred) X p(a department is transferred / a department has already been transferred)

---

[19] **Logic Note**. Notice that the multiplicative rule applies to a situation that has the logical form of the "conjunction," discussed in Unit II under deductive reasoning with connectives.

92

Thus, there is a 7% (33% X 20%) chance that both you and your neighbor are transferred to the new office complex.

Self-Test: Section IV.B.4 (answers are given on page 132)

The problems below require you to apply the multiplicative rules of probability. Try to determine the correct answer before reading the explanation given at the end of the manual.

1. While driving to work, Loukas' car breaks down and is towed to a nearby garage. After examining the car, a mechanic tells Loukas that three parts need to be replaced for the car to run properly. After receiving the estimate, Loukas tells the mechanic that he cannot afford to have the car repaired at the price quoted. Eager to get business, the mechanic tells Loukas that he can save money by using rebuilt parts, but warns that each rebuilt part has a 90% chance of working. After thinking about it for a while, Loukas estimates that there is about a 70% chance that his car will run properly with the rebuilt parts. As a result, he decides to borrow money and get new parts put in. Do you agree with Loukas' assessment that there is about a 70% chance that his car will run properly with the rebuilt parts? Justify your answer by applying the multiplicative rule for independent events.

2. Jennifer has recently graduated from college with a degree in marketing. She receives a call from her friend Bob who tells her about a job he has applied for at a prestigious marketing firm. The firm is hiring two associates at the entry level. Excited about the prospect of working with Bob, Jennifer applies for the job. After one week goes by, Jennifer calls the personnel department at the marketing firm to inquire about her application. She is told that, including her and Bob's applications, four people have applied for the two jobs and that no other applications will be accepted.

   Applying the multiplicative rule of probability, Jennifer determines that there is a 25% chance (50% X 50%) that she and Bob will be offered positions at the marketing firm. Do you agree with Jennifer's assessment that there is a 25% chance that she and Bob will both get a job offer? Justify your answer applying the multiplicative rule for dependent events.

Section IV.B.5. Additive Rules of Probability

The ***additive rule for independent events*** states that the probability that at least one of a number of independent events will occur is equal to the sum of their individual probabilities. For example, imagine you join a scuba diving group. As a practice, two members are randomly paired each time the group meets to go diving. Understanding the dangers of scuba diving, you are concerned about being paired with a novice diver. You find out that 35% of the group members are novice divers, 50% of the members are intermediate divers, and 15% of the members are expert divers. In probability, these events are represented as:

p(novice) = 35%
p(intermediate) = 50%
p(expert) = 15%

The probability of being paired with either an intermediate diver or an expert diver is determined by applying the additive rule for independent events as follows:

p(intermediate or expert) = p(intermediate) + p(expert)

Thus, there is a 65% chance (50% + 15%) that you will be paired with either an intermediate or an expert diver.

When two events are not independent, the ***additive rule for dependent events*** is used to determine the probability that at least one of a number of dependent events will occur. For example, imagine you are in charge of recruiting for a local police force. An analysis shows that the most successful officers either have a college degree or have military experience. Concerned that there will not be enough qualified people to fill the openings, you decide to survey people interested in becoming an officer to assess how many people would meet the criterion of having a college degree or having military experience. You find that 60% of those interested in becoming an officer have a college degree and 40% have military experience.

Applying the additive rule for independent events would suggest that all people who are interested in becoming officers would be qualified. However, because you are dealing with two related events (that is, some people will have both a college degree and military experience), it is necessary to subtract the joint probability of having a college degree and having military experience. Imagine that the results of your survey suggest the following

94

joint probabilities for each possible combination of having or not having a college degree and military experience.

	Military Experience	No Military Experience	Total
College Degree	30%	30%	60%
No College Degree	10%	30%	40%
Total	40%	60%	100%

Where:

p(college degree, military experience) = 30%
p(college degree, no military experience) = 30%
p(no college degree, military experience) = 10%
p(no college degree, no military experience) = 30%

Applying the additive rule for dependent events you find the following:

p(college degree or military experience) =
p(college degree) + p(military experience) - p(college degree, military experience)

Thus, there is a 70% chance (60% + 40% - 30%) that a person interested in becoming an officer has either a college degree or military experience.[20]

Self-Test: Section IV.B.5 (answers are given on page 132)

The problems below require you to apply the additive rules of probability. Try to determine the correct answer before reading the explanation given at the end of the manual.

1. Donna is not feeling well and decides to schedule a medical examination at one of two doctors' offices. Both offices have 20 doctors working at all times. In the past, Donna has had a number of problems with general practitioners and residents. As a result, she prefers to see internists or specialists whenever possible. Unfortunately, the policy at both offices is that a patient is treated by the first available doctor. Donna decides to call both offices to find out how many general practitioners, residents, internists, and specialists work at each office. She gets the following information.

	General Practitioner	Resident	Internist	Specialist
Office A	45%	5%	35%	15%
Office B	35%	20%	40%	5%

Given this information, at which office should Donna schedule an appointment given her preference for internists and specialists? Justify your answer by applying the additive rule for independent events.

---

[20] **Logic Note**. Notice that situations in which the additive rule is used have the logical form of the *alternation*, discussed in Unit II under deductive reasoning with connectives.

95

2. During a morning meeting, Sharon's supervisor tells her that she must rent temporary office space by the end of the business day. Sharon contacts a real estate agent and tells her that she is interested in renting an office that either has ample parking space or is near public transportation. In order to narrow the search, the real estate agent tells Sharon the percentage of offices with ample parking space and the percentage of offices near public transportation in each town in the area. After hearing her options, Sharon decides that the best place to rent an office is in Milltown because 50% of the offices have ample parking space and 50% of the offices are near public transportation. On the basis of this information, Sharon determines that there is a 100% chance that the office will either have ample parking space or be near public transportation. Sharon tells the real estate agent she will rent an office in Milltown. Do you agree with Sharon's assessment that the office is guaranteed either to have ample parking space or to be near public transportation? Justify your answer by applying the additive rule of probability for dependent events.

Section IV.B.6. Summary

This part of the unit has concentrated on ways to increase the likelihood that you will make accurate inferences in everyday life. You should go back and re-read relevant sections if you feel unsure about any of the principles outlined above. The next part of the unit will outline some of the common mistakes people make when estimating the likelihood of events.

Part IV.C. Biases in Statistical Reasoning and Estimations of Probability

While the rules of statistical reasoning and probability described above can increase the likelihood that an estimate will be accurate, people often fail to apply them. Instead, people apply *heuristics* or rules-of-thumb when making estimates that an event will occur. The term heuristic refers to the speculative formulation of a solution to a problem. While the use of heuristics can result in effective actions, heuristics can also lead people to ignore or misinterpret useful information. This part of the unit describes the most common heuristics and shows how the use of heuristics can result in inaccurate estimates when you perform your job.

Section IV.C.1. Availability

Which is more likely, being killed in a car crash or being killed in a plane crash? If you use the *availability* heuristic, your response to this question would be based on the event that is most easily retrieved from memory. Since the media are more likely to report incidents of plane crashes, people using the availability heuristic are more likely to retrieve memories of a plane crash in which people were killed than they are of a car crash in which people were killed. However, a person is more likely to be killed in a car crash than in a plane crash.

The use of the availability heuristic can result in violations of a number of the rules of statistical reasoning. For example, imagine you are asked to estimate the probability that a person will be married by the time he or she is 25 years old. If you use the availability heuristic, your estimate would be based on the percentage of marriages among people you know (that is, friends and relatives) in their early to mid-twenties because these examples easily come to mind. A violation of the law of large numbers can occur if you only know a few people who are in their early to mid-twenties. A violation of the rule of sample representativeness can occur because your sample is likely to consist of people who are similar on a number of characteristics, such as ethnicity, religion, educational level, and geographic location. Each of these factors is related to the age at which a person gets married.

Section IV.C.2. Representativeness

Representativeness refers to the tendency to assign an event to a category based on the degree to which the event resembles other members of the category. For example, you may assume that a person driving a Porsche is wealthy. It also can refer to the tendency to believe that event "A" resulted from process "B." For example, you may assume that a person does not have a job because he or she is lazy.

Perhaps the most prevalent examples of the use of the representativeness heuristic are *stereotypes*. Stereotypes are general descriptions of a category that allow us to make quick decisions based on a limited amount of available information. When stereotypes lead to inaccurate estimates, it is usually because two variables are perceived to go together even

97

though a relationship between them does not exist. This tendency has been termed *illusory correlation*. For example, a common stereotype is that accountants are boring. Despite this stereotype, there is no evidence that there is a correlation between being an accountant and being boring.

The use of the representativeness heuristic can result in the violation of a number of the rules of statistical reasoning. For example, imagine you are asked if John will be a good student. You are told that John plays three sports during the school year. If you hold the stereotype that athletes are poor students, you will probably predict that John will not be a good student. In this example, a violation of the law of large numbers can occur if your stereotype of athletes' scholastic performance is based on a few observations of athletes in a classroom. A violation of the rule of sample representativeness can occur because stereotypes often result in *selective perception* when observing events of interest. That is, people have a tendency to notice or remember events that are consistent with their stereotype, and ignore events that are inconsistent with their stereotype. As a result, your estimate may be based on a restricted sample consisting of observations confirming your stereotype.

Section IV.C.3. Dilution

Dilution refers to the tendency to make a conservative estimate of the probability that an event will occur when irrelevant information is provided along with relevant information. For example, imagine you are searching for a primary care physician in your Health Maintenance Organization (HMO). An HMO representative recommends a young doctor whose office is located close to your home. The representative tells you that the doctor graduated at the top of her class from a prestigious medical school. Given this information you would probably predict that the doctor is very competent and make an appointment to see her. When you arrive at her office, you find that the doctor is wearing clothes that do not match and has not combed her hair. As a result of the doctor's appearance, your confidence in her ability to practice medicine is decreased. In this case, the doctor's appearance has diluted your estimate of her qualifications to practice medicine.

Dilution can result in a violation of the rule of sample validity. This occurs because irrelevant information is used to make an estimate. In the example presented above, considering the doctor's physical appearance when making an estimate of her ability to practice medicine may result in an erroneous conclusion. An evaluation of the doctor's ability to practice medicine should be based on factors related to the medical profession rather than her physical appearance.

Section IV.C.4. Anchoring and Adjustment

Anchoring and adjustment refers to the tendency to make conservative adjustments from a reference point as new information is provided. An example of anchoring and adjustment can be found in the television game show "The Price is Right." In this game, four contestants are asked to estimate the price of a prize. The contestant with the closest estimate without going over the actual price proceeds to a game in which he or she can win other prizes. Typically, the remaining three contestants use the first contestant's estimate of the price as a reference point, adjusting their estimates only slightly from this point.

Anchoring and adjustment can result in a failure to recognize the regression to the mean phenomenon when the initial reference point is extreme. For example, imagine you ask 50 people if they agree that 90% of teenagers in the United States play a musical instrument. Most people would say they feel fewer than 90% of the teenagers in the United States play a musical instrument. Now imagine that you ask another 50 people if they feel 1% of the teenagers in the United States play a musical instrument. In this instance, most people would say they feel that more than 1% of the teenagers in the United States play a musical instrument. However, if people given a reference point of 90% are asked to give a specific estimate of how many teenagers play a musical instrument, most will give an estimate less than, but close to 90%. Similarly, the people given the reference point of 1% will most likely give an estimate of more than, but close to 1%.

Section IV.C.5. Order Effect

Order effect refers to the tendency to make estimates based solely on initial or recent observations. For example, imagine that Agent Smith has recently been assigned to work in your sector, and makes a costly mistake on his first day on the job. When conducting a performance appraisal, you may determine that Agent Smith performed less than adequately even if his performance was acceptable for most of the review period. Now imagine you are asked to conduct a performance appraisal for Agent Jones. During the review period, Agent Jones has performed at an adequate level. However, in the past week, she has apprehended an unusually high number of illegal aliens. You may be inclined to give Agent Jones a high rating for the entire review period based on her most recent performance, even though her performance for the entire period was adequate.

The order effect can lead people to violate the law of large numbers and the rule of sample representativeness. It can also result in a failure to recognize the regression to the mean phenomenon. Estimates based on early or recent observations violate the law of large numbers because only a few observations are considered. For example, only considering Agent Smith's initial level of performance when making your evaluation restricts your sample of observations to one day. A violation of the rule of sample representativeness can occur because your sample would not include performance in all areas, at different times, and under different conditions. Finally, the order effect can result in a failure to recognize the regression to the mean phenomenon when initial (or recent) observations are extreme. For example, suggesting Agent Jones get a promotion on the basis of her performance over the last week of the review period would be inappropriate because her performance will most likely return to the level of the preceding weeks.

Section IV.C.6. Ignoring Relative Frequency

Ignoring relative frequency refers to the tendency to make estimates based on observed frequencies rather than on relative frequencies. This occurs when information on nonoccurrences is ignored or not available. For example, imagine you are interested in buying a four-wheel drive vehicle. Due to an extremely harsh winter the previous year, orders for the vehicle you are interested in purchasing are greater than the number of vehicles produced. You go to two dealerships to see if they have the vehicle available. Dealership A claims to be getting 10 vehicles in each month, while dealership B claims to be getting 20 vehicles in each month.

At first, it may appear that you would have a better chance of getting the vehicle from dealership B. However, an examination of the number of people purchasing the vehicle at each dealership suggests that, on average, 20 people purchase the vehicle at dealership A, while an average of 60 people purchase the vehicle at dealership B. Given this information, you would determine that you are more likely to get the vehicle from dealership A (10 vehicles for 20 orders) than from dealership B (20 vehicles for 60 orders). Therefore, it is important to consider the relative frequency rather than absolute frequency when determining probabilities.

Ignoring relative frequency can result in an erroneous estimate of the base rate. In the example above, the base rate of getting a vehicle at dealership A is 50%, while the base rate of getting the vehicle at dealership B is 33%. If you ignore the relative frequency, you would most likely estimate that the base rate of getting the vehicle is greater at dealership B than at dealership A simply because dealership B will be receiving more vehicles during a given month.

Section IV.C.7. Concrete Information

Concrete information refers to the tendency to give observed information more weight than abstract information, even if the abstract information is more reliable. For example, imagine you are the chief of police in a major U.S. city. You are interested in determining whether the crime rate has changed over the past year. Anecdotal evidence from two of your top officers suggests that crime has gone down. However, a recently released FBI report based on all crime reported in the city suggests that the crime rate in your city has increased 5%. You may be tempted to give the opinions of the officers more weight than the FBI report simply because their reports are based on first-hand experience.

Favoring concrete information can result in violations of the law of large numbers and the rule of sample representativeness. In the example above, a violation of the law of large numbers can occur because the estimate is based on the experiences of a very small percentage of all possible police officers in the city. A violation of the rule of sample representativeness can occur because it is unlikely that the officers are exposed to all

100

neighborhoods in the city. On the other hand, the FBI report is based on all crime reported in the city, regardless of neighborhood.

Section IV.C.8. Gambler's Fallacy

Gambler's fallacy refers to the tendency to overestimate the probability of the occurrence of an event not previously observed. For example, imagine you and a friend have planned a fishing trip during the upcoming weekend. You are concerned that it may rain, noting to your friend that it rains 60% of the weekends during this time of year. In fact, it has rained during each of the past five weekends. Always the optimist, your friend states it probably will not rain because "we are due for a sunny weekend."

In this example, the gambler's fallacy has resulted in your friend's misuse of the multiplicative rule for independent events. The gambler's fallacy occurs because people focus on the probability of a sequence of events rather than the probability of the occurrence of a single, independent event. Applying the multiplicative rule for independent events, you would find that there is a 5% chance that it will rain during 6 consecutive weekends (.6 X .6 X .6 X .6 X .6 X .6). However, since the probability that it will rain during any individual weekend is independent of whether it has rained during previous weekends, there is still a 60% chance that it will rain during the weekend of your fishing trip.

The gambler's fallacy is also referred to as the *Monte Carlo fallacy*. It got this name in 1913 when a roulette wheel at a Monte Carlo casino came up red 26 times in a row. After the 13th spin, people began betting large sums of money on black, working under the assumption that the probability of the ball landing on a red number 14 times in a row is infinitesimal. Unfortunately, they failed to consider that the probability of an outcome during each spin of the wheel is independent of previous outcomes. As a result, many people lost large sums of money by betting on black during the next 13 spins of the wheel.

Section IV.C.9. Misperceptions about Equiprobability

Misperceptions about equiprobability refers to the tendency to define incorrectly the probability that two or more events will occur as equal when in fact they are not. For example, imagine you have a friend coming in from out of town for the weekend. You plan a number of outdoor activities and want to determine the probability that it will be sunny during both days of the weekend. On any given day, there is a 50% chance that it will be sunny and a 50% chance that it will rain.

When determining the probability that it will be sunny on both days, many people consider the possible combinations of weather during the two days without respect to the order in which the sunny and rainy days occur. Using this approach, they assume there is an equal chance that it will be sunny both days, raining both days, and sunny one day and raining one day. This results in an estimate that there is a 33% chance that it will be sunny on both days during the weekend. However, the belief that each of the combinations has the same probability of occurring is a faulty assumption. In all, there are four possible combinations of sunny and rainy days over a period of two days:

	First Day	Second Day
1.	Sun	Sun
2.	Sun	Rain
3.	Rain	Sun
4.	Rain	Rain

Since there are four possible combinations, there is a 25% chance (1/4) that any individual combination will occur. Examining the table above, you will notice that there is a 25% chance that it is sunny during both days (#1), and a 25% chance that it is raining during both days (#4). In order to determine the probability of having one day of sun and one day of rain, you must apply the additive rule for independent events. There is a 25% chance that it is sunny during the first day and raining during the second day (#2), and a 25% chance that it is raining during the first day and sunny during the second day (#3). Applying the additive rule for independent events, you find that probability of having one sunny day and one rainy day during the weekend is equal to 50% (25% + 25%). In this case, the misperception of equiprobability would result in an underestimate of the probability that it is sunny one day and raining on one day. Notice that the probability that it is sunny one day and raining one day (50%) is twice as large as the probability that it is sunny both days (25%) or raining both days (25%).

Section IV.C.10. Overestimating Conjunctive Events

Overestimating conjunctive events refers to the tendency to overestimate the probability that two events will occur. For example, Tversky and Kahneman (1982) presented people with the following description:

Linda is 31 years old, single, outspoken, and very bright. She majored in philosophy. As a student, she was deeply concerned with issues of discrimination and social justice, and also participated in antinuclear demonstrations. Please check off the most likely alternative:

☐ Linda is a bank teller.
☐ Linda is a bank teller and is active in the feminist movement.

Nearly 90% of the respondents said that Linda is more likely to be a feminist bank teller than a bank teller. However, according to the multiplication rule for independent events, the probability that two events will occur (that is, being a bank teller and a feminist) cannot be greater than the probability of either event alone. Thus, the probability that Linda is a bank teller is necessarily greater than the probability that she is a feminist bank teller.

The conjunction fallacy results in a violation of the multiplicative rule, and tends to become more profound as the number of events involved increases. This can be shown using the example of the rebuilt car parts presented in problem 1 of the self-test for section IV.B.4

covering the multiplicative rules of probability. Remember that in the problem, the three rebuilt car parts each had a 90% chance of working correctly, resulting in a 73% chance that the car will work correctly with all three rebuilt parts. However, if five rebuilt parts were used (each with a 90% chance of working correctly) there is a 59% chance that the car will work correctly.

Section IV.C.11. Summary

In this part of the unit, heuristics that often lead to erroneous estimates of probability were presented. When making an evaluation, consider whether you have used one of the heuristics described above. If you have used one of the heuristics, think about the rules of statistical reasoning and probability that it violated, and determine its impact on the accuracy of your assessment. Below are tables which list heuristics described above and the rules of statistical reasoning and probability they violate.

Table 1. Biases in Statistical Reasoning

Bias	Law of Large Numbers	Sample Representativeness	Regression to the Mean	Sample Validity
Anchoring and Adjustment			X	
Availability	X	X		
Concrete Information	X	X		
Dilution				X
Order Effect	X	X	X	
Representativeness	X	X		

Table 2. Biases in Estimating Probabilities

Bias	Base Rate	Multiplicative Rules	Additive Rules
Gambler's Fallacy		X	
Ignoring Relative Frequency	X		
Misperceptions about Equiprobability			X
Overestimating Conjunctive Events		X	

References for Unit IV

Kahneman, D., & Tversky, A. (1982). On the study of statistical intuitions. Cognition, 11, 237-251.

Unit V - Posttest for Manual of Job-Related Thinking Skills

The following passage describes a set of facts. The passage is followed by eight conclusions. Read the passage and then decide whether each conclusion is:

T) **true**, *which means that you can infer the conclusion from the facts given; or*

F) **false**, *which means that the conclusion is contrary to the facts given; or whether there is*

I) **insufficient information to decide**, *which means that there is insufficient information for you to determine whether the facts imply the conclusion or are contrary to the conclusion.*

A staff member who is responsible for scheduling meetings at a district office needs to be aware of certain practices and requirements within the district. For example, all naturalization ceremonies in the district are scheduled for Wednesdays and Thursdays. Of course, no naturalization ceremonies are closed to the public. However, some meetings that are closed to the public are held in the district director's conference room.

1. The only events held on Wednesdays and Thursdays are naturalization ceremonies. (T / F / I)

2. Any event that is scheduled for Tuesday is not a naturalization ceremony. (T / F / I)

3. Some naturalization ceremonies are not held on Wednesday or Thursday. (T / F / I)

4. All naturalization ceremonies are open to the public. (T / F / I)

5. Some meetings held in the district director's conference room are closed to the public. (T / F / I)

6. Some events held in the district director's conference room are not naturalization ceremonies. (T / F / I)

7. No events that are held on Wednesdays or Thursdays are closed to the public. (T / F / I)

8. Some naturalization ceremonies are not held in the district director's conference room. (T / F / I)

104

The following passage describes a set of facts. The passage is followed by eight conclusions. Read the passage and then decide whether each conclusion is:

T) **true**, *which means that you can infer the conclusion from the facts given; or*

F) **false**, *which means that the conclusion is contrary to the facts given; or whether there is*

I) **insufficient information to decide**, *which means that there is insufficient information for you to determine whether the facts imply the conclusion or are contrary to the conclusion.*

When an Adjudications Officer interviews an applicant for a benefit, such as a green card, certain prescribed procedures are followed. If the information provided by the applicant meets the legal criteria for approval, and only if it meets these criteria, the application is approved on the spot. If the information does not meet the criteria, either the applicant is asked to supply additional information or the application is denied. If the Adjudications Officer suspects fraud, a Special Agent is asked to join the interview.

9. If a Special Agent is not asked to join the interview, then the applicant is not suspected of fraud. (T / F / I)

10. If the information provided by the applicant does not meet the legal criteria, the application is not approved on the spot. (T / F / I)

11. If the applicant is not asked to supply additional information, then the information already provided meets the legal criteria. (T / F / I)

12. If the application is approved on the spot, then the information provided meets the legal criteria. (T / F / I)

13. Even if the information provided by the applicant meets the legal criteria, the application often is not approved on the spot. (T / F / I)

14. A certain individual's application was not approved on the spot; as a result, a Special Agent was asked to sit in on the interview with this individual. (T / F / I)

15. If the Adjudications Officer does not suspect fraud, a Special Agent is not asked to join the interview. (T / F / I)

16. If the information provided by an applicant does not meet the legal criteria for approval but the application is not denied, then the Adjudications Officer has asked for more information. (T / F / I)

The following passage describes a set of facts. The passage is followed by eight conclusions. Read the passage and then decide whether each conclusion is:

T) **true***, which means that you can infer the conclusion from the facts given; or*

F) **false***, which means that the conclusion is contrary to the facts given; or whether there is*

I) **insufficient information to decide***, which means that there is insufficient information for you to determine whether the facts imply the conclusion or are contrary to the conclusion.*

Security measures have been developed to protect laptop computers used at DHS. Unauthorized access is one security concern. If individuals without proper DHS clearance obtain access to DHS computers or data, it is considered to be unauthorized access. As one form of protection, all DHS laptops should have access control software. The physical security of laptops, particularly during travel, is another concern. If a laptop computer is checked as baggage, it must be secured in a specialized storage container.

17. Some of the computers that should have access control software are DHS laptops. (T / F / I)

18. If a computer is an DHS laptop, then it should have access control software. (T / F / I)

19. The only computers at DHS that need to have access control software are laptops. (T / F / I)

20. If a person who did not have a proper DHS clearance obtained access to data from a laptop, but not to the laptop itself, this would not be considered unauthorized access. (T / F / I)

21. If there was no unauthorized access to an DHS laptop, that means that no individuals without an DHS clearance obtained access to the laptop or its data. (T / F / I)

22. If an DHS laptop is not being checked as baggage, it does not need to be secured in a specialized storage container. (T / F / I)

23. All computers that must be secured in specialized storage containers also have access control software. (T / F / I)

24. No DHS laptop should be without access control software. (T / F / I)

The following passage describes a set of facts. The passage is followed by eight conclusions. Read the passage and then decide whether each conclusion is:

T) **true**, *which means that you can infer the conclusion from the facts given; or*

F) **false**, *which means that the conclusion is contrary to the facts given; or whether there is*

I) **insufficient information to decide**, *which means that there is insufficient information for you to determine whether the facts imply the conclusion or are contrary to the conclusion.*

In Sector X, illegal immigrants enter the country through one of two areas--either through a border crossing on one of several highways or by crossing areas of rough terrain away from the highways. A study of activity in this sector revealed that nearly all of the illegal immigrants under the age of 16 that were apprehended were intercepted at the highway border crossings. It was also found that nearly all illegal immigrants apprehended while crossing the areas of rough terrain were 16 years of age or older. During the last month of the study, the number of illegal aliens apprehended in rough terrain was twice as great as the number intercepted at highway border crossings.

25. An illegal alien intercepted in rough terrain was most likely to be 16 years of age or older. (T / F / I)

26. If an illegal alien was not apprehended in an area of rough terrain, then the alien was not under the age of 16. (T / F / I)

27. An illegal alien apprehended at a highway border crossing was more likely to be under the age of 16 than to be 16 years of age or older. (T / F / I)

28. Of the illegal aliens who were 16 years of age or older and who were apprehended while trying to enter this sector, nearly all attempted to cross the area of rough terrain.(T / F / I)

29. If an illegal immigrant under the age of 16 is apprehended, it is most likely to be at a highway border crossing. (T / F / I)

30. During the last month of the study, an illegal alien apprehended while entering this sector was more likely to be 16 years of age or older than to be under the age of 16. (T / F / I)

31. During the last month of the study, an illegal immigrant 16 years of age or older who was apprehended was more likely to have been apprehended at a highway border crossing than in rough terrain. (T / F / I)

32. During the last month of the study, an illegal alien who was not apprehended was most likely to have crossed the border at a highway border crossing. (T / F / I)

End of Posttest. Check your answers against those on pages 134-138.

Unit I - Answers to Self-Test and Manual of Job-Related Thinking Skills Pretest

Unit I

1. basic
2. certain
3. complete
4. probabilistic
5. incomplete
6. induction

Manual of Job-Related Thinking Skills Pretest

1. True. This conclusion can be inferred from the second sentence of the paragraph, which says that none of the criminal cases resulting from apprehensions by the Border Patrol at Station X last month were narcotics cases. Since none of the criminal cases was a narcotics case, it follows that no narcotics cases were among the criminal cases resulting from apprehensions.

2. Insufficient information. The third sentence states that there were a few criminal cases involving alien smuggling that were not referred to another agency. The paragraph does not tell us anything about criminal cases that were referred to another agency. The paragraph does not give us enough information to conclude that there were such cases.

3. True. The first sentence says that only narcotics cases are referred to DEA. The second sentence says that none of the criminal cases resulting from apprehensions last month were narcotics cases. From that information, we can conclude that none of the criminal cases resulting from apprehensions at Station X last month were referred to the DEA.

4. True. Since all narcotics cases are referred to DEA, it must be that any case that is not referred to DEA is not a narcotics case.

5. False. This statement contradicts the second sentence of the paragraph, which says that *none* of the criminal cases resulting from apprehensions by the Border Patrol in Station X last month were narcotics cases. If the second sentence is true, then it cannot be true that some criminal cases apprehended last month by the Border Patrol in Station X were narcotics cases.

6. True. This answer can be inferred from the first sentence of the paragraph. Since all narcotics cases resulting from apprehensions by the Border Patrol are referred to the DEA, it must be that none of them remain unreferred to DEA.

7. Insufficient information. The paragraph does not provide us any information about cases that were referred to other agencies. It only tells us about cases that were *not* referred to other agencies. We cannot tell from the paragraph whether or not any cases were referred to another agency.

8. True. This conclusion can be inferred from information in the second and third sentences. The third sentence says that a few criminal cases resulting from apprehensions last month involved alien smuggling. We know that these cases did not involve narcotics because the second sentence says that none of the criminal cases resulting from apprehensions last month were narcotics cases.

9. True. This conclusion can be inferred from the second sentence, which says that an alien must have either a border crossing card or a resident alien card or a passport. If an alien does not have one of these documents, he or she must present one of the other two types of document.

10. True. This conclusion can be inferred from the first sentence of the paragraph, which states that if aliens do not present themselves for inspection at a designated port of entry, they cannot enter the U.S.A. legally. From this statement, we can conclude that presenting oneself for inspection is an absolute requirement for entry. Therefore, if an alien was allowed to enter the U.S.A., then the alien must have met that requirement.

11. Insufficient information. Although the first sentence states that presenting oneself for inspection is a requirement for entry, we cannot conclude that M.N. was allowed to enter simply because she presented herself at the designated port of entry. She might not have met other requirements for entry, as stated in the second sentence. Therefore, the paragraph does not give us sufficient information to conclude that she would be allowed to enter.

12. Insufficient information. The paragraph does not give us information about all aliens who entered at this port of entry for the purpose of shopping. We know that all people who entered with a border crossing card were either visiting family or shopping. However, some people who came for shopping may have presented another type of document (for example, a passport).

13. True. The paragraph tells us that in the week J.T. entered, every alien who had a border crossing card entered either to visit family or to shop. J.T. had a border crossing card and he was not coming to shop. Therefore, he must have entered to visit his family.

14. False. This conclusion is false because it contradicts the information in the first sentence, which says that if aliens do not present themselves at a designated port of entry, they cannot enter the U.S.A. legally.

15. Insufficient information. The paragraph does not give us any information about the characteristics of aliens who entered without a border crossing card.

16. Insufficient information. The paragraph tells us that aliens must present themselves at a designated port of entry and have one of three documents in order to enter the country legally. This is not sufficient information for us to conclude that if an alien does not present himself or herself at a port of entry, then he or she does not have one of the three documents.

17. True. The third sentence says that there were several apprehensions that involved extensive pursuit by local authorities. From this sentence we can conclude that some cases that involved pursuit by local authorities resulted in apprehensions. We know from the second sentence that all apprehended persons took voluntary departure. Therefore, we can conclude that some cases that involved extensive pursuit by local authorities resulted in the voluntary departure of aliens.

18. False. This information contradicts the information in the first and second sentences. The first sentence says that an illegal alien cannot both take voluntary departure and be deported. According to the second sentence, all apprehended aliens took voluntary departure, which leads to the conclusion that *none* was deported.

19. Insufficient information. The third sentence says that several apprehensions involved extensive pursuit by local authorities. This does not give us sufficient information to conclude that all apprehensions involved such pursuit.

20. True. Three cases involved pursuit to a crossroads where the individual either turned left or was picked up by a vehicle, or both. Two of the individuals were not picked up by a vehicle. Therefore, they must have taken the left turn.

21. True. This conclusion is equivalent in meaning to the third sentence of the paragraph, which says that "there were several apprehensions that involved extensive pursuit by local authorities."

22. Insufficient information. The paragraph does not tell us if all apprehensions were the result of extensive pursuit by local authorities (see explanation for question 19). Therefore, we cannot conclude that everyone who took voluntary departure was apprehended as the result of such pursuit.

23. True. This conclusion is equivalent in meaning to the third sentence of the paragraph. Since some apprehensions did involve extensive pursuit by local authorities we can say that these same apprehensions did not occur without such pursuit.

24. False. This conclusion contradicts the eighth sentence, which says that in these three cases, the individuals had either turned left or been picked up by a vehicle, or both.

25. Insufficient information. There is insufficient information to estimate the probability that an illegal alien crossing the bridge when the train is present will be apprehended. According to the last sentence of the first paragraph, although aliens are apprehended when the train is present, the sensor is of no use in signaling the presence of people under such circumstances. Furthermore, the passage does not tell the proportion of aliens that are apprehended and thus we cannot estimate the probability that an individual alien will be apprehended while crossing the bridge if a train is present.

26. True. The third sentence states that if there is no train, 70% of sensor signals lead to apprehensions of illegal aliens. Therefore, if an Agent responds to such a signal, there is a 70% chance that an alien will be apprehended.

27. Insufficient information. The passage does not give us information about the number of aliens who cross the bridge without being apprehended. Therefore, we do not know the likelihood that people who crossed without being apprehended did so when the train was present.

28. True. This conclusion is correct because the information in the passage allows us to conclude that in an average week at least 70 people are apprehended crossing when the train is not present and 10 people are apprehended crossing when the train is present. Therefore, at least seven-eighths of the people are apprehended while crossing in the absence of the train. Since the overwhelming majority are apprehended crossing while the train is absent, it is very likely that this was the case for group A.

29. Insufficient information. There is no information that allows us to conclude how often trains are present. Although many more aliens are apprehended when the train is absent, it could be simply that many more try to cross the bridge when the train is absent.

30. True. The last sentence of the first paragraph states that apprehensions are made when the train is present. Therefore, it cannot be true that no apprehensions occur when a train is present.

31. False. This is an incorrect statement of the likelihood that a sensor signal will lead to an apprehension of an illegal alien when a train is not present. From the information in the paragraph we must conclude that there is only a 70% chance of an apprehension.

32. Insufficient information. The passage does not give information about the number of illegal aliens who attempt to cross the bridge and that number cannot be inferred from any other information in the passage. Therefore, there is no way to estimate whether more aliens attempted to cross when no train was present or when a train was present.

Unit II - Answers to Self Tests

1. True
2. True
3. Some weapons are guns.
   Anything that is not a weapon is not a gun.
4. No weapons are guns.
   Some guns are not weapons.
5. Invalid
6. Valid
7. Invalid
8. Valid

Part II.A

Section II.A.1

1. (not a set) rewritten as a set: "individuals who are listening"
2. a set
3. (not a set) rewritten as a set: "hazardous materials (or acts)"
4. (not a set) rewritten as a set: "forms that are completed and filed"
5. a set
6. computer software, user friendly products
7. law enforcement personnel, people who carry guns
8. Mexicans, people who were deported
9. Border Patrol Agents, people who speak Spanish
10. Service employees, people who are responsible for immediately reporting any allegation of misconduct

Section II.A.2

1.

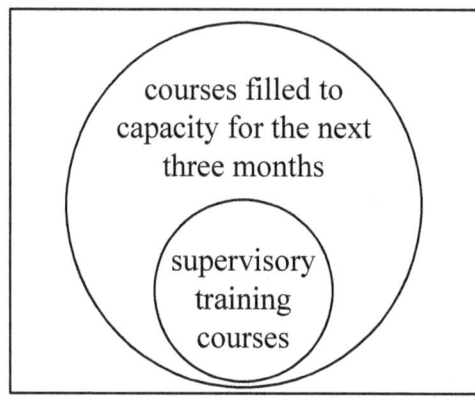

Every supervisory training course is filled to capacity for the next three months.

112

2.

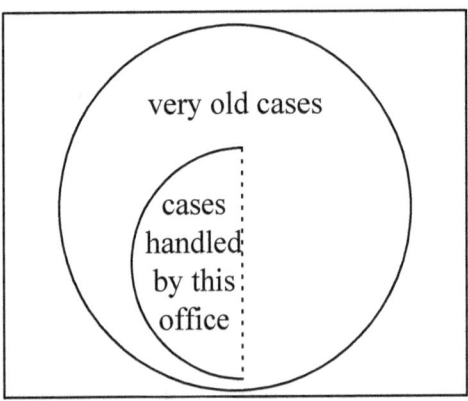

Some of the cases being handled by this office are very old.

3.

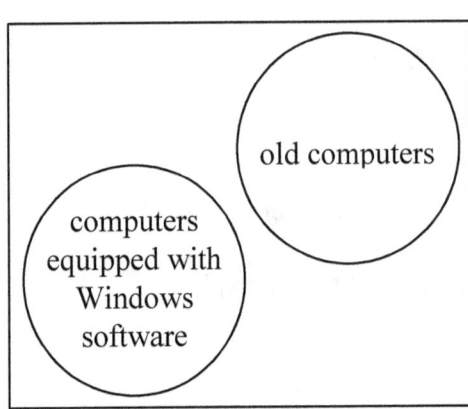

None of the old computers is equipped with Windows software.

4.

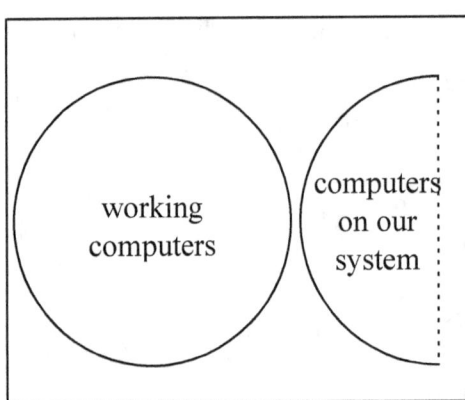

A few computers on our system are not working.

Section II.A.3

1a. False. This conclusion contradicts the information in the original statement.

1b. True. If all members of our staff have mailboxes at the front desk, then it must be true that there are some people who have mailboxes at the front desk who are members of our staff.

1c. Insufficient information. The original statement does not tell us if the members of our staff are the only people who have mailboxes at the front desk. It may be that members of some other staff also have mailboxes in the same place. (This form is the *converse*, which in this case, you may recall, is a common reasoning mistake, or illogical bias.)

1d. True. Since all members of our staff have mailboxes at the front desk, it must be true that anyone who does not have a mailbox there is not a member of our staff. (This is the form called the *contrapositive*, which was referred to in Logic Note 2.)

2a. Insufficient information. The original statement tells us about every supervisory training course in the next three months, but it does not tell us about every course that is filled to capacity. Therefore, we do not have enough information to conclude that every course that is filled to capacity for the next three months is a supervisory training course. (This form is again the *converse,* which in this case is a reasoning error.)

2b. False. This conclusion is contrary to the information in the original statement.

2c. True. Since all the supervisory training courses are filled to capacity for the next three months, it must follow that none of them is filled to less than capacity. This conclusion represents a double negation of the original statement. (This form is called the *obverse*, which was referred to in Logic Note 3.)

2d. True. Since all the supervisory training courses are filled to capacity for the next three months, it must follow that any course that is not filled to capacity is not a supervisory training course. (This form is called the *contrapositive*, which was referred to in Logic Note 2.)

Section II.A.4

1a. False. This conclusion contradicts the information in the original statement.

1b. True. If none of the new Jeeps are being deployed to Station 1, it must be true that none of the vehicles being deployed to Station 1 is a new Jeep. The two sets "new Jeeps" and "vehicles being deployed to Station 1" are completely excluded from each other. This is the form known as the *converse.*

1c. True. Since none of the new Jeeps are being deployed to Station 1, it must be true that all of the new Jeeps are among the vehicles that are not being deployed to Station 1. This conclusion represents a double negation of the original statement. (This form is called the *obverse*, which was referred to in Logic Notes 3 and 4.)

1d. False. This conclusion is contrary to the information in the original statement.

2a. False. This conclusion is contrary to the information in the original statement.

2b. True. Since none of the Assistant Chiefs will be able to attend the meeting, it follows that none of the people who will attend the meeting are Assistant Chiefs. This conclusion is valid because the two sets (Assistant Chiefs, people who will be able to attend the meeting) are completely separate from each other. This form is called the *converse*.

2c. False. This conclusion contradicts the information in the original statement.

2d. True. Since none of the Assistant Chiefs will be able to attend the meeting, it follows that all of the Assistant Chiefs are unable to attend the meeting. This conclusion represents a double negation of the original statement. (This form is called the *obverse*, which was referred to in Logic Notes 3 and 4.)

Section II.A.5

1a. True. Since some DHS employees are trained in the use of firearms, it must be true that there are some people trained in the use of firearms that are employees of DHS. This is the form known as the *converse*.

1b. Insufficient information. The original statement referred to only *some* DHS employees. It does not give us enough information to draw a conclusion about *all* DHS employees.

1c. False. This conclusion contradicts the information in the original statement.

1d. True. Since some DHS employees are trained in the use of firearms, it must be true that there are some DHS employees that are not untrained in the use of firearms. This conclusion represents a double negation of the original statement (the *obverse*).

2a. Insufficient information. The original statement only gives information about some Canadian citizens. It does not tell us about whether or not there are some Canadian citizens who are ineligible to work in the United States.

2b. True. Since some Canadian citizens are eligible to work in the United States, it must be true that these Canadian citizens are not ineligible to work in the United States. This conclusion represents a double negation of the original statement (the *obverse*) and is synonymous with it.

2c. Insufficient information. The original statement does not give information about all Canadian citizens, so we do not have enough information to know if this conclusion is true or not.

2d. True. Since some Canadian citizens are eligible to work in the United States, it must be true that some people who are eligible to work in the United States are Canadian citizens. This form is the converse.

Section II.A.6

1a. False. This conclusion clearly contradicts the information in the original statement.

1b. Insufficient Information. The original statement said that I received some documents that were not in acceptable form. It said nothing about whether or not I also received some documents that *were* in acceptable form.

1c. True. This statement is equivalent to the original statement. It represents a double negation of the original statement (the form called the *obverse).*

1d. Insufficient Information. The original statement only said I received some documents that were not in acceptable form. We do not know whether or not that refers to all the documents that were received. It might be that I received some documents that *were* in acceptable form.

2a. Insufficient information. The original statement said that there were some computers in our office that cannot run the new software. That statement does not tell us which computers *can* run the software or indeed if there are any computers that can run it. If you concluded that this statement is true, you have fallen into an illogical bias (a prevalent reasoning error). This form is the *converse* of the original statement.

2b. Insufficient information. The original statement does not give us information about *all* the computers in our office. The statement only mentions "some" computers. Therefore, we cannot draw a conclusion that applies to all of the computers in the office.

2c. Insufficient information. The original statement says that some computers in our office cannot run the new software. That information is not sufficient in itself to let us conclude that there are some computers in our office that *can* run the software. If you chose "True" for this conclusion, you committed an illogical bias, a common reasoning mistake.

2d. False. This conclusion contradicts the information in the original statement.

Section II.A.7

1a. Insufficient information. We know it is not true that none of the computers can run the new software. Therefore, it must be true that at least some of them can run the software. However, we do not have enough information to conclude that *all* of the computers in our office can run the new software.

1b. True. See explanation for *a* above.

1c. Insufficient information. See explanation for *a* above. Just as we do not have enough information to know if *a* is true, we also do not have enough information to know if *c* is true. Given the initial statement, either *a* or *c* must be true. However, we do not have enough information to know which is true.

2a. False. If it is not true that some of the employees in our office received awards last year, then it must be true that none did. It certainly is false to conclude that *all* of them did.

2b. True. See *a* above.

3a. Insufficient information. Since it is not true that all of the passengers boarding the plane have proper documentation of U.S. citizenship, it must be that some of them do not have such documentation. However, we do not have enough information to conclude that *none* of the passengers have proper documentation.

3b. Insufficient information. See *a* above. Even though it is not true that all passengers boarding the plane have proper documentation, it may be that some of them do. However, we do not have sufficient information to draw that conclusion.

3c. True. See *a* above.

4a. True. If it is not true that some DHS managers have not completed the training course, then it must be true that all of them have completed it.

4b. False. If it is not true that some DHS managers have not completed the training course, then it is clearly also not true that none of them have completed the course.

Part II.B

Section II.B.1

For each pair of statements below, underline the middle term and then write a valid conclusion relating the other two terms.

1.   Premise 1: All <u>DHS employees</u> are Federal Government employees.
            Premise 2: All ICE employees are <u>DHS employees</u>.
            Possible Conclusion: All ICE employees are Federal Government employees. *or*
                       Some Federal Government employees are ICE employees.

            Explanation: The set "ICE employees" is completely included in the set "DHS employees," which is in turn completely included in the set "Federal Government employees." The second conclusion can be deduced from the first.

2.   Premise 1: No <u>Canadian citizens</u> are U.S. citizens.
            Premise 2: All citizens of Quebec are <u>Canadian citizens</u>.
            Possible Conclusion: No citizens of Quebec are U.S. citizens. *or*
                       No U.S. citizens are citizens of Quebec.

            Explanation: The first premise says that the set of Canadian citizens is completely separate from the set of U.S. citizens. The second premise says that all citizens of Quebec are completely included in the set of Canadian citizens. Therefore, all citizens of Quebec must be completely excluded from the set of U.S. citizens. The converse of this statement (see Section II.A.4) is also valid.

3.   Premise 1: No District 1 staff has <u>completed the new training</u>.
            Premise 2: All recently hired adjudicators have <u>completed the new</u> training.
            Conclusion: No recently hired adjudicators are on the District 1 staff. *or*
                    No one on the District 1 staff is a recently hired adjudicator.

            Explanation: According to the second premise, all recently hired adjudicators have completed the new training. However, from the first premise, it can be deduced that no one who has completed the new training is on the District 1 staff. Therefore, it must be true that none of the recently hired adjudicators are on the District 1 staff. The converse of this statement (see Section II.A.4) is also valid.

4.   Premise 1: Some agents are <u>trained in Advanced CPR</u>.
            Premise 2: All <u>employees trained in Advanced CPR</u> passed the Basic CPR course.
            Conclusion: Some agents have passed the Basic CPR course. *or*
                    Some people who passed the Basic CPR course are agents.

Explanation: From the second premise we know that all employees trained in Advanced CPR passed the Basic CPR course, and from the first premise we know that some agents are trained in Advanced CPR. Therefore, we can conclude that some agents have passed the Basic CPR course. We can also conclude the valid converse (see Section II.A.5), that some people who passed the Basic CPR course are agents.

5. Premise 1: All <u>ICE vehicles</u> are listed in the vehicle database.
    Premise 2: Some Department of Homeland Security vehicles are not <u>ICE vehicles</u>.
    Conclusion: From the information contained in these premises, no conclusion is possible about the relationship between DHS vehicles and vehicles listed in the ICE vehicle database.

    Explanation: No valid conclusion can be drawn from these two premises. The second premise tells us that some DHS vehicles are not ICE vehicles. The first premise tells us that all ICE vehicles are listed in the ICE vehicle database, but it gives us no information about non-ICE vehicles. Therefore, we can draw no further conclusion about DHS vehicles.

6. Premise 1: <u>All persons born in the U.S.A.</u> are U.S. citizens.
    Premise 2: <u>All persons born in the U.S.A.</u> can get social security cards.
    Conclusion: Some people who can get social security cards are U.S. citizens. *or*
               Some U.S. citizens can get social security cards.

    Explanation: From the second premise, we can conclude that some people who can get social security cards are born in the U.S. When that information is combined with the information in the first premise--that all persons born in the U.S. are U.S. citizens--we can conclude that some people who can get social security cards are U.S. citizens. We can also conclude the valid converse (see Section II.A.5), that some U.S. citizens can get social security cards.

Section II.B.2

1. Invalid. The term "Federal Government employees" is distributed in the conclusion but not in the premises--a violation of rule 5.

2. Valid. The conclusion is negative in accordance with rule 2. The middle term is distributed in premise 2 (rule 4). Both sets are distributed in the conclusion and in the premises (rule 5).

3. Valid. Premise 1 refers to only part of a set, so the conclusion refers to only part of a set (rule 7). Both premises are affirmative, so the conclusion is affirmative (rule 3). The middle term is distributed in premise 2 (rule 4). Neither term is distributed in the conclusion or in the premises (rule 5).

4. Invalid. The premises are both affirmative but the conclusion is negative--a violation of rule 3; also, the term "under the jurisdiction of the DHS" is distributed in the conclusion but not in the premises--a violation of rule 5.

Section II.B.3

1. There is insufficient information to draw this conclusion. From the converse of the second premise (see Section II.A.3), assuming that there were people who failed to qualify last week, we can conclude that there were some employees who must qualify with their firearm this week. These people are the employees who failed to qualify last week. However, there may be other employees who need to qualify this week (for example, employees who were not tested last week). Therefore, we can only conclude that *some* of the employees who have to qualify with their firearm this week are not Special Agents.

   A valid conclusion is: Some employees who have to qualify with their firearm this week are not Special Agents.

2. There is insufficient information to draw this conclusion. It could be that there are other entries into the service system besides requests for computer assistance. This erroneous conclusion stems from committing the illogical bias of assuming that the converses of premise 1 and premise 2 are valid (see Section II.A.3). We only have enough information to conclude that *some* entries in the computer system are Help Desk requests and that *some* Help Desk requests are for computer assistance.

   A valid conclusion is: Some entries into the service system are requests for computer assistance.

3. Valid.

4. Invalid. No valid conclusion about the space assigned to Jim and the space on this floor can be drawn because the two premises only refer to undefined parts of sets. There is no way to tell if the space assigned to Jim is the same Logistics office space that is on this floor.

Part II.C

Section II.C.1

1a. The Department of Homeland Security both <u>confers benefits</u> and <u>enforces laws</u>.

1b. Not a conjunction

1c. To be successful, a teletraining instructor <u>must maintain "eye contact" with the viewers</u> and <u>must involve viewers in interactive exercises</u>.

1d. A complete computer set-up includes a <u>processor</u>, a <u>display</u>, a <u>keyboard</u>, and a <u>mouse</u>.

1e. Not a conjunction

2a. The new vehicles do not have four-wheel drive.

2b. It is not the case that both Agent López and Agent Johnson are on annual leave today.

2c. It is not true that the agency will use both classroom training and computer-based training in the future.

2d. Neither you nor I will attend the meeting.

2e. It is not true that the ceremony will be canceled if it rains.

Section II.C.2

1a. If <u>you contribute to the Combined Federal Campaign through payroll deduction</u>, then
                       (antecedent)

    <u>there is a record of a deduction on your biweekly earnings statement</u>.
          (consequent)

1b. If <u>an international flight arrives</u>, <u>Inspectors process the arriving passengers</u>.
    (antecedent)   (consequent)

1c. <u>You can take the advanced supervisory course</u> only if <u>you have taken the basic</u>
      (antecedent)   (consequent)

    <u>supervisory course</u>.

1d. This is not a conditional. It is an alternation, which will be described in the next section.

1e. Whenever <u>an entire office undergoes a move</u>, <u>there is an inevitable period of</u> disruption.
         (antecedent)   (consequent)

2a. If you are a CBP Inspector, then you work for DHS.

2b. When someone is hired into the Border Patrol, that person always attends training in Glynco.

2c. A person can receive e-mail messages only if his or her computer is connected to a network.

2d. If you study a foreign language enthusiastically, you will develop a good vocabulary in that language.

3a. Insufficient information. This conclusion is based on the invalid converse of the conditional. This conclusion rests on the assumption that if a computer has a modem, it was purchased for someone on the A-Team. The original conditional sentence does not permit us to draw that conclusion.

3b. True. Because John's computer was purchased for the A-Team, it does have a modem.

3c. True. Because all computers purchased for the A-Team have modems, any computer that does not have a modem was not purchased for the A-Team. (This form is the contrapositive; see Logic Note 1.)

3d. Insufficient information. The original conditional statement only refers to computers that were purchased for the A-Team. It says nothing about computers purchased for other teams. They may or may not have modems.

4a. Insufficient information. The conditional sentence only tells what will happen if we request the same spending level as last year. It does not say what will happen if we request a higher level.

4b. True. The original conditional statement told us that our budget would be approved if we requested the same spending level as last year. Since our budget was not approved, we must not have requested the same spending level. (This form is the contrapositive; see Logic Note 1.)

4c. False. This statement contradicts the original conditional statement.

4d. True. If the original conditional statement is true, then this statement is true. This statement says that the antecedent of the conditional is true. Therefore, the consequent must also be true.

Section II.C.3

1a. Conditional

1b. Disjunction

1c. Alternation

1d. Biconditional

1e. Conditional

2a. Insufficient information. It is possible that the Jeep has both a faulty starter and bad spark plugs. The fact that it has a faulty starter does not rule out the possibility that it has bad spark plugs.

2b. Insufficient information. The Jeep might have only one of the two problems. Having bad spark plugs does not necessarily mean that it also has a faulty starter.

2c. True. If the Jeep does not have bad spark plugs, it must have a faulty starter. The original statement said that the Jeep had either one or the other of these two problems. If it does not have one of the problems, it must have the other one.

2d. True. See explanation for *c*.

3a. True. The branch does not have both a color printer and a black-and-white printer. If the branch has a color printer, it does not have a black-and-white printer.

3b. Insufficient information. Although the branch does not have both a color printer and a black-and-white printer, we do not know for sure if the branch has either of these two pieces of equipment. Therefore, if a branch does not have one piece of equipment, the same branch may or may not have the other piece.

3c. Insufficient information. See explanation for *b*.

3d. False. This must be false because a branch does not have both a color printer and a black-and-white printer.

Section II.C.4

1. Insufficient information. The form represents the invalid converse of the compound conditional (If p, then q and r; q and r, therefore p). The original statement said that if the consultant's recommendations were implemented, then we would achieve two results. However, the statement did not say that the only way to achieve these results was to implement the consultant's recommendations. It could be that we would achieve the same results by pursuing another course of action. Therefore, knowing that we achieved these results is not enough to let us conclude that the consultant's recommendations were implemented.

2. True. According to the conditional statement, implementing the consultant's recommendations would lead to certain results. If the results are not achieved, then the consultant's recommendations must not have been implemented.

3. True. The antecedent of the conditional is true. Therefore, the consequent must be true.

4. Insufficient information. Just stating that a result was achieved is not sufficient to let us conclude that the consultant's recommendations were implemented. That result could have been achieved for another reason.

5. True. This says that the plan to be implemented will not achieve the results expected from implementing the consultant's recommendations. Therefore, the plan must not include implementing these recommendations. (This conclusion is the contrapositive; see note 3.)

124

Unit III - Answers to Self-Tests

Part III.A

1. True
2. False
3. True
4. False
5. False
6. True
7. True

8a. Deductive, good reasoning
8b. Inductive, poor reasoning
8c. Deductive, good reasoning
8d. Inductive, good reasoning

Part III.B

Section III.B.1

1a. Unknown. Since many illegal aliens are not "observed," the staff officer will need to draw conclusions about these unobserved individuals and also project future trends, which cannot be known at present.

1b. Known. Personnel records contain this information for all DHS employees.

1c. Known. Total expenditures and expenditures for travel are documented for each fiscal year.

1d. Unknown. The recruitment specialist has no way to find out about the reading habits of all college seniors. She must draw conclusions based on college seniors who apply for DHS jobs.

2a. Correct inference. Ninety percent of the new agents in Sector X are new hires. Therefore, Agent A.B. is very likely to be a new hire.

2b. Incorrect inference. Eighty percent of the new agents in Sector Y are new hires. Therefore, it is not very likely that C.D. transferred from another sector. There is only a 20% chance that this happened.

2c. Incorrect inference. The paragraph does not give information about what percent of all new Border Patrol hires are in Sector Y. Therefore, we cannot say that it is "likely" that E.F. works there.

2d. Correct inference. Ten percent of the new agents in Sector X transferred from another sector.

3a. Correct inference. Since three-fourths of the nonofficer crew members are not from Norway, it must be that one-fourth are from Norway. Therefore, any nonofficer crew member has a one-fourth chance of being from Norway.

3b. Correct inference. See explanation for *a*.

3c. Incorrect inference. We do not know the proportion of the total crew that are officers. Therefore, we cannot estimate the chances that a Norwegian crew member is an officer.

3d. Incorrect inference. Since all of the officers are from Norway, any crew member who is not from Norway is also not an officer (this is a deductive conclusion).

4a. Correct inference. There is a 50% chance that there would be a tour for a new employee, but there is also a chance (probability unknown) that there would be a tour for official visitors.

4b. Incorrect inference. The paragraph does not tell us about the relative frequency of tours for new employees and for official visitors. Therefore, we cannot say if a tour on Monday is more likely to be for a new employee or for official visitors.

4c. Correct inference. Since the probability was 50% that there would be a tour for a new employee, an upper limit of 50% is set on the chance that there would not be a tour. Depending on the frequency of official visitors, the chance that there would be no tours might be even lower.

4d. Correct inference. On any Monday there was a 50% chance that there would be a new employee. Therefore, there was a 50% chance that there would not be a new employee.

5a. Correct inference. The paragraph tells us that all of the computer equipment, which constitutes 30% of the items, has not been declared surplus. It is possible, perhaps even likely, that there are other items that have not been declared surplus. Therefore, there is at least a 30% chance that a randomly selected piece of equipment has not been declared surplus.

5b. Correct inference. Since the probability is at least 30% that a randomly selected piece of equipment has not been declared surplus, then the probability that it *has* been declared surplus cannot exceed 70%.

5c. Incorrect inference. None of the computer equipment has been declared surplus. Therefore, any piece of equipment that has been declared surplus could not be a piece of computer equipment.

5d. Incorrect inference. There is at least a 30% chance that this piece of equipment is computer equipment, given that 300 pieces of computer equipment had not been declared surplus.

6a. Not an inductive generalization. Squares are defined as having four sides.

6b. An inductive generalization based on the observations of patterns of moss growth.

6c. An inductive generalization based on observations of the harm done to bodies by exposure to radiation.

6d. Not an inductive generalization. As of 1996, 50 governmental entities had been legally declared states.

Section III.B.2

1a. Correct inference. A randomly selected employee from the work site had a 30% chance of being an undocumented alien. If the person was an undocumented alien, then he or she was not from a North, South, or Central American country. In addition, other workers from the site might not be from a North, South, or Central American country. Therefore, there is at least a 30% chance that a randomly selected employee at that site was not from a North, South, or Central American country.

1b. Incorrect inference. Based on the second sentence in the paragraph, one must conclude, by deduction, that no employee from that site who was from a North, South, or Central American country was an undocumented alien.

1c. Correct inference. Since at least 30% of the employees (the undocumented aliens) are not from a North, South, or Central American country, the probability that a randomly selected employee was from the Americas was not more than 70%.

1d. Incorrect inference. Although none of the undocumented aliens was from a North, South, or Central American country, the country of origin of the other 70% of the employees is unknown.

127

2a. Incorrect inference. The paragraph does not give us sufficient information to draw a conclusion about the exact distribution of new and "holdover" furniture in the redecorated area.

2b. Correct inference. Only 20% of the items of furniture in the visitors area before redecoration were made of wood, which was required for use after redecoration. Therefore, there was only a 20% chance that an item of furniture that was used before the redecoration could have been used after the redecoration.

2c. Correct inference. Eighty percent of the furniture in the visitors area before the redecoration did not have wood frames and thus did not meet the requirement for furniture in the redecorated area. In addition, pieces of furniture from before the redecoration may not be used for other reasons. Thus, there is at least an 80% chance that an item of furniture in the room before redecoration would not be used after the redecoration.

3a. Correct inference. A case from Agent Z's caseload had a 50% chance of being a case of document counterfeiting and thus being investigated vigorously. In addition, it is possible, no doubt very likely, that there were other types of cases that were investigated vigorously. Thus, the chance that a randomly selected case is investigated vigorously is 50% or greater.

3b. Correct inference. All cases that are vigorously investigated have not failed to yield a successful prosecution. Since this case has at least a 50% chance of being investigated vigorously, it also has at least a 50% chance of not failing to produce a successful prosecution.

3c. Incorrect inference. The chance that this case was not investigated vigorously is no more than 50%, but it could be less than 50% (compare to the explanation for *a*).

3d. Incorrect inference. The chance that this case was prosecuted unsuccessfully is not more than 50%, but it could be less than 50% (compare to explanation for *b*).

Part III.C

Section III.C.1

1a. Correct conclusion. Vehicle A is a typical vehicle apprehended while transporting illegal aliens. Therefore, according to the paragraph, there is a 20% chance that it was stopped for speeding.

1b. Incorrect conclusion. Vehicle B was transporting illegal aliens but was not apprehended. The paragraph does not give us any information about the probability that such a vehicle was not stopped for speeding.

1c. Correct conclusion. If vehicle A had a 20% chance of being stopped for speeding, it had an 80% chance of not being stopped for speeding. These two probabilities are the complements of each other.

1d. Incorrect conclusion. The paragraph does not give us information about the universe of vehicles stopped for speeding. We only know that some of them were transporting illegal aliens. We do not know what the percentage is.

2a. Incorrect conclusion. The paragraph does not give us information about the record of returns for all books signed out for purposes other than specific work projects. Therefore, we cannot assign a definite value to the probability that such a book will be returned on time.

2b. Correct conclusion. The paragraph tells us that of all books returned on time, 70% were signed out for use on specific work projects. Therefore, we can estimate that 700 of 1000 such books were returned on time.

2c. Correct conclusion. The paragraph tells us that if a book was signed out for use on a specific work project, there is a 70% chance that it will be returned on time. Therefore, we can estimate that 350 of 500 such books will be returned on time.

2d. Incorrect conclusion. The paragraph does not give us information on all the books that were not returned on time. Therefore, we cannot estimate how likely it is that such a book was signed out for a reason other than a work project.

Section III.C.2

1a. Correct conclusion Since one-tenth of the cases are criminal aliens, all of whom are not detained at the DHS facility, there is a lower limit on the percentage of cases that would not be detained there and hence on the probability that any case involved someone who was not detained there.

1b. Correct conclusion. This conclusion is the complement of the conclusion in *a*. If the chances of not being detained in an DHS detention facility are at least 10%, then the chances of being detained at such a facility can be no more than 90%.

1c. Incorrect conclusion. This conclusion is false because the probability that a case concerns a noncriminal alien is exactly .90, which is 1 minus .10 (the probability that a case concerns a criminal alien).

2a. Correct conclusion. Since there is a 90% chance that there was a record of a special deduction on an employee's earnings statement, there is a 10% chance that there is no special deduction. This sets a lower limit on the chance that an employee did not contribute to the Combined Federal Campaign through payroll deduction. It is assumed that there could be a special deduction on the earnings statement for some other reason (such as an allotment for a bond purchase), so the probability of not contributing could be greater than .10).

2b. Incorrect conclusion. This is not an accurate statement of the probability that a randomly selected employee did contribute to the Combined Federal Campaign through payroll deduction. That probability is somewhere in the range of 0 to .90.

2c. Correct conclusion. This is the complement of the probability that a randomly selected employee did have a special deduction on the earnings statement.

3a. Incorrect conclusion. This conclusion is false because the correct probability is *exactly* 25%.

3b. Correct conclusion. This is the complement of the correct version of answer *a*.

3c. Correct conclusion. The employee worked more than eight hours on one-fourth of her work days and these are the only days eligible for overtime.

4a. Incorrect conclusion. The 40% of the work stations that were not fixed had received neither the new hardware nor the upgraded software. If they had received either of those two items, the problems would have been corrected.

4b. Incorrect conclusion. There is insufficient information to draw this conclusion. The 60% of the work stations that were fixed would have been fixed if they had received either of these new items. There is no way to tell if any of them had received both items.

4c. Correct conclusion. The 40% of work stations that were not fixed clearly had received neither the new hardware nor the upgraded software. There is also the possibility that some of the work stations whose problems had been corrected had been fixed through some other means (for example, reconfiguration by a skilled technician). That is why the probability is at least .40.

Unit IV - Answers to Self-Tests

Part IV.A

Section IV.A.1

1. While it is tempting to give the information provided by the two coworkers more weight than the results of the survey, it is unlikely that the coworkers' friends represent all people who own the car John is interested in purchasing. According to the law of large numbers, a survey of 1,000 car owners is more likely to be representative of the population of car owners than are the coworkers' friends. Since the results of the survey suggest that most people are satisfied with the car, John should consider purchasing the car.

2. In this problem, Center B is more likely to have days on which at least 7.5% of the claims processed are incorrect. According to the law of large numbers, small samples are more likely to provide extreme observations than large samples. Therefore, over the course of the year, Center B is more likely to have days in which 7.5% of the claims processed are incorrect. Similarly, Center B is also more likely to have days on which 2.5% or fewer of the claims processed are incorrect. However, when the number of incorrect claims processed at each plant is averaged over the course of a year, both Center A and Center B are likely to process incorrect claims 5% of the time. This occurs because days on which very few incorrect claims are processed at Center B will be offset by days on which many incorrect claims are processed.

Section IV.A.2

1. The sample used in the newspaper poll is more likely to be accurate for a number of reasons. First, even though the poll conducted by the newspaper excluded voters who do not have telephones, it is more likely to be representative of the population of voters because it was randomly selected. On the other hand, the local news program poll only included viewers of the program. Second, the local news program poll required viewers to pay $.50 in order to participate. This restricted the local news program poll sample to viewers who were willing to pay $.50 to participate in the poll.

This example highlights the fact that we are often forced to draw conclusions from flawed samples. Understanding the rules of statistical reasoning helps us to maximize our chance of drawing an accurate conclusion even when we are provided with less than ideal samples (in some circumstances you may feel you cannot draw an accurate conclusion given the samples provided).

2. You may have noticed that both samples are small and violate the law of large numbers. Ideally, Lisa should continue to collect information before making an evaluation. However, in order to focus on sample representativeness, assume that Lisa cannot collect more information. In this case, Lisa should use her coworker's sample to estimate the percentage of employees in the district willing to work overtime because his sample included employees working during many shifts in key areas within the district. On the other hand, Lisa's sample was restricted to employees working during one shift in a specific area within the district. This reduces the probability that her sample reflected the population of employees in the district.

Section IV.A.3

1. Laura was right to be skeptical of the effectiveness of the course. Since the class consisted of a group of students who performed poorly on the test, the increased scores may be the result of regression to the mean. Remember, a student's test score is a function of two factors: his or her actual ability and chance factors. Even if his or her ability remains constant, a student's score will most likely be different on the second administration of the test because chance factors impact his or her score on both administrations. The first time a student who scored extremely low took the test, chance factors were likely to have had an negative effect on performance (e.g., the student may have been sick when taking the test). The impact of chance factors during the second administration of the test is not likely to be as negative, resulting in the student's receiving a higher test score.

   Stronger evidence would have been provided if the class had consisted of low, average, and high scoring students. Laura could be confident in the effectiveness of the course if all students scored higher on the second administration of the test, regardless of their score on the first administration. On the other hand, if only low scoring students improved their test scores, the increase could be attributed to regression to the mean.

2. Since the relationship between the comedian's stand-up routine and his acting ability is not perfect, Greg and Jane should not be surprised by the comedian's performance. For the most part, good stand-up comedians will be good actors. Occasionally, a good stand-up comedian will be only a fair actor. Therefore, Greg and Jane should be disappointed (they just spent $7.00 each to see the movie), but not surprised that the stand-up comedian was not a great actor.

Section IV.A.4

1. Julia's claim that the most expensive stereo system is best violates the rule of sample validity. The difference in price could be due to a number of factors other than quality. For example, a stereo system may be more expensive because of higher shipping costs. Therefore, Julia's claim that most expensive stereo system is better may be incorrect. She should have based her assessment on attributes known to be related to quality.

2. While the sample used in the survey of overall satisfaction satisfies the law of large numbers and sample representativeness, David should not use the results to draw conclusions about employee satisfaction with pay. Overall satisfaction can be attributed to a number of factors other than pay including the nature of the job, relationships with coworkers, and the quality of supervision. Therefore, using overall job satisfaction ratings to assess satisfaction with pay may lead David to draw an erroneous conclusion.

Part IV.B

Section IV.B.4

1. While each individual part has a 90% chance of working, all three parts must be working correctly simultaneously for the car to run properly. According to the multiplicative rule for independent events, the probability of the car running properly is determined by multiplying the individual probability that each part will work (90% X 90% X 90%). As a result, there is a 73% chance that the car will run properly when using the three rebuilt parts. Therefore, Loukas' estimate was correct.

2. Jennifer failed to take into account the fact that the probability of a person's being offered a position decreases after a job offer has been given to another person. As a result, Jennifer incorrectly applied the multiplicative rule for independent events to determine the probability that she and Bob will be offered positions at the marketing firm. In this problem, there is a 50% chance of getting a job offer given that no job offers had been given. However, there is only a 33.33% chance of getting a job offer given that one job offer has already been made (3 applicants for 1 job opening). Applying the multiplicative rule for dependent events would have resulted in Jennifer's determining that there is a 16.7% (50% X 33.33%) chance that she and Bob will both get job offers from the marketing firm.

Section IV.B.5

1. Using the additive rule for independent events, Donna should choose to make an appointment at Office A. Given the information provided, there is a 50% chance (35% + 15%) that Donna will be assigned to either an internist or a specialist at Office A. On the other hand, there is only a 45% chance (40% + 5%) that Donna will be assigned to either an internist or a specialist at Office B.

2. Much to Sharon's dismay, she may find that her assessment was wrong. Remember that the additive rule for dependent events must be applied when events are related. While there are many possible combinations of the office having ample parking space and/or being near transportation, below is a table containing one.[21]

	Near Transportation	Not Near Transportation	Total
Ample Parking	25%	25%	50%
Limited Parking	25%	25%	50%
Total	50%	50%	100%

Where:

p(ample parking, near transportation) = 25%
p(ample parking, near transportation) = 25%
p(limited parking, not near transportation) = 25%
p(limited parking, not near transportation) = 25%

Sharon was correct in estimating that there is a 50% chance the office has ample parking and a 50% chance the office is near public transportation. However, there is a 25% chance that the office has both ample parking and is near public transportation, a probability common to both events. In order to account for the overlap between the two events, it is necessary to subtract the probability of the office's having ample parking and being close to public transportation. This results in the following formula:

p(ample parking or near transportation) =
p(ample parking) + p (near transportation) - p(ample parking , near transportation)

Thus, there is a 75% chance (50% + 50% - 25%) that the office has ample parking space or is near public transportation.

---

[21] There are a number of possible combinations of an office having ample parking space and/or being near transportation. For example, if most offices that provide ample parking are located near public transportation, a table such as the following might result:

	Near Transportation	Not Near Transportation	Total
Ample Parking	10%	40%	50%
Limited Parking	40%	10%	50%
Total	50%	50%	100%

Notice that, while the percentages inside the table have changed, the total percentages have remained the same (50% of offices are located near public transportation and 50% of the offices provide ample parking).

Unit V - Answers to Manual of Job-Related Thinking Skills Posttest[22]

1. Insufficient information. The second sentence in the paragraph states that all naturalization ceremonies in the district are scheduled for Wednesdays and Thursdays. This is not sufficient information to allow us to conclude that naturalization ceremonies are the *only* events held on Wednesdays and Thursdays. It could be that other events are also held on those days. (Deductive reasoning with two sets)

2. True. This conclusion follows from the second sentence of the paragraph. Since all naturalization ceremonies in the district are held on Wednesdays and Thursdays, an event that is held on any day other than Wednesday or Thursday is not a naturalization ceremony. (Deductive reasoning with two sets)

3. False. This conclusion contradicts the information in second sentence. (Deductive reasoning with two sets)

4. True. The third sentence in the paragraph states that no naturalization ceremonies are closed to the public. This is the same as saying that all naturalization ceremonies are open to the public. (Deductive reasoning with two sets)

5. True. This conclusion is equivalent in meaning to the fourth sentence, which states that some meetings that are closed to the public are held in the district director's conference room. (Deductive reasoning with two sets)

6. True. From the fourth sentence we can conclude that some meetings held in the district director's conference room are closed to the public. In the third sentence, we learn that no naturalization ceremonies are closed to the public. From these two statements we can conclude that at least some events held in the district director's conference room -- the ones that are closed to the public -- are not naturalization ceremonies. (Deductive reasoning with three sets)

7. Insufficient information. This conclusion goes beyond the information in the paragraph. The paragraph permits us to conclude that some events held on Wednesday or Thursday -- the naturalization ceremonies -- are not closed to the public. It does not permit us to conclude that no events held on those days are closed to the public. You might be led to draw this erroneous conclusion if you interpreted the second sentence of the paragraph as meaning that the only events held on Wednesdays and Thursdays are naturalization ceremonies. (Deductive reasoning with three sets)

---

[22] The type of thinking skill used in each question is given in parentheses at the end of each question.

8. Insufficient information. Question 6 represented the valid conclusion that some events held in the district director's conference room are not naturalization ceremonies. However, we are not justified by this conclusion or by any other information in the paragraph in concluding that some naturalization ceremonies are *not* held in the district director's conference room. (Deductive reasoning with three sets)

9. True. The last sentence of the paragraph states that if an Adjudications Officer suspects fraud when interviewing an applicant for a benefit, a Special Agent is asked to join the interview. From this statement we can conclude that if no Agent is asked to join the interview, the applicant is not suspected of fraud. (Deductive reasoning with connectives)

10. True. The second sentence says that an application is approved on the spot if and only if the information provided by the applicant meets the legal criteria. From this statement we can conclude that if the information does not meet legal criteria, the application is not approved on the spot. (Deductive reasoning with connectives)

11. Insufficient information. We cannot draw the conclusion that, if an applicant is not asked to supply additional information, the information already provided meets the legal criteria. As stated in the third sentence, another course of action -- denial of the application -- is also possible when the information does not meet the criteria. (Deductive reasoning with connectives)

12. True. The second sentence tells us that an application is approved on the spot only if the information provided meets legal criteria. Therefore, we can conclude that if an application is approved on the spot, the information provided must meet the legal criteria. (Deductive reasoning with connectives)

13. False. This contradicts the second sentence of the paragraph, which states that if the information provided meets legal requirements, the application is approved on the spot. (Deductive reasoning with connectives)

14. Insufficient information. The paragraph does not give us enough information to draw this conclusion. The last sentence says that a Special Agent is asked to join the interview if fraud is suspected. The paragraph does not indicate that an Agent would be called anytime an individual's application fails to be approved on the spot. (Deductive reasoning with connectives)

15. Insufficient information. The paragraph does not say that an Agent is asked to join an interview *only* in cases of suspected fraud. There may be other situations in which a Special Agent is asked to join an interview. Therefore, we do not have enough information to decide that this conclusion is either true or false. (Deductive reasoning with connectives)

16. True. The third sentence states that if the information provided by an applicant does not meet legal criteria, then one of two actions is taken: either the applicant is asked to provide additional information or the application is denied. Therefore, if the information does not meet legal criteria for approval and the application is not denied, it must be that the Adjudications Officer has asked for more information. (Deductive reasoning with connectives)

17. True. The fourth sentence of the paragraph says that all DHS laptops should have access control software. From this statement, we can conclude that some of the computers that should have access control software are DHS laptops. (Deductive reasoning with two sets)

18. True. This conclusion is equivalent to saying that all DHS laptops should have access control software, which is the same as the information in the fourth sentence of the paragraph. (Deductive reasoning with two sets and connectives)

19. Insufficient information. The paragraph says that all DHS laptops should have access control software. It does not state that laptops are the only type of computers that should have this software. It could be that desktop computers also should have access control software. (Deductive reasoning with two sets)

20. False. The third sentence of the paragraph clearly says that unauthorized access occurs when individuals without proper clearance obtain access to computers or data. Access to data alone is thus considered unauthorized access. (Deductive reasoning with connectives)

21. True. The third sentence says that unauthorized access occurs when individuals without proper clearance obtain access to computers or data. Therefore, if there has been no unauthorized access, it must mean that no individuals without proper clearance obtained access either to DHS computers or to DHS data. (Deductive reasoning with connectives)

22. Insufficient information. The last sentence of the paragraph says that if a laptop computer is being checked as baggage, it must be secured in a specialized storage container. However, the paragraph does not tell us whether or not a specialized container is also needed when the computer is not being checked as baggage. (Deductive reasoning with connectives)

23. Insufficient information. We are able to conclude that some computers that must be secured in specialized storage containers also have access control software; these are DHS laptops that are being checked as baggage. However, we do not have enough information to make the general conclusion that *all* computers that must be secured in specialized storage containers also have access control software. We might reach this overly general conclusion if we erroneously concluded that all computers that must be

secured in specialized storage containers are DHS laptops. But the paragraph does not give us the information to draw that conclusion. (Deductive reasoning with sets and connectives)

24. True. The fourth statement says that all DHS laptops should have access control software. This is equivalent to saying that no DHS laptop should be without access control software. (Deductive reasoning with connectives)

25. True. The third sentence states that nearly all illegal immigrants apprehended while crossing the areas of rough terrain were 16 years of age or older. Therefore, an illegal alien intercepted in rough terrain is most likely to be 16 years of age or older. (Inductive reasoning with two sets)

26. Insufficient information. The second sentence says that nearly all illegal immigrants under the age of 16 were intercepted at highway border crossings rather than in areas of rough terrain. Therefore, it is clear that some illegal immigrants under the age of 16 were intercepted away from areas of rough terrain. If an illegal alien was not apprehended in an area of rough terrain, we cannot necessarily conclude that the alien was not under the age of 16. (Inductive reasoning with sets and connectives)

27. Insufficient information. Although we know that nearly all illegal immigrants under the age of 16 were intercepted at highway border crossings, we do not know if individuals under the age of 16 constitute the majority of illegal aliens intercepted at these crossings. Therefore, we do not have enough information to conclude that an illegal alien apprehended at a highway border crossing was more likely to be under the age of 16 than to be 16 years of age or older. (Inductive reasoning with two sets)

28. Insufficient information. Although the third sentence tells us that nearly all the illegal immigrants apprehended while trying to cross the area of rough terrain were 16 years of age or older, we do not know if this group constituted the majority of individuals 16 years of age or older who were apprehended while trying to enter the sector. Therefore, we do not have enough information to conclude that nearly all illegal aliens 16 years of age or older apprehended while trying to enter this sector tried to cross the area of rough terrain. (Deductive reasoning with two sets)

29. True. The second sentence says that nearly all of the illegal immigrants under the age of 16 who were apprehended were intercepted at the highway border crossings. Therefore, we can conclude that if an illegal immigrant under the age of 16 is apprehended, it is most likely to be at a highway border crossing. (Inductive reasoning with two sets)

30. True. During the last month of the study, according to the last sentence of the paragraph, the number of illegal immigrants apprehended in rough terrain was twice as great as the number apprehended at highway border crossings. Since those

apprehended while crossing areas of rough terrain are nearly all 16 years of age or older, it follows that an illegal alien apprehended while entering this sector was more likely to be 16 years of age or older than to be under the age of 16 during the last month of the study. (Inductive reasoning with three sets)

31. False.   Since apprehensions were twice as high in the rough terrain as at border crossings, and since those apprehended in rough terrain were nearly all 16 years of age or older, it follows that an illegal immigrant 16 years of age or older was more likely to be apprehended in rough terrain. (Inductive reasoning with three sets)

32. Insufficient information.   The paragraph does not give any information about illegal aliens who were not apprehended. (Inductive reasoning with two sets)